MIDLIFE MISADVENTURES IN CUBA

THEIR LOVE LIFE IS FAILING. WILL AN ADVENTUROUS VACATION EXPLODE INTO CHAOS, OR BRING THEM CLOSER TOGETHER?

KEVIN J. D. KELLY

GET THE PREQUEL BOOK FOR FREE

Sign up and get *MIDLIFE MISADVENTURES IN MARGATE* and a bonus book, all for free. They are exclusive to the newsletter. Find out what happened before Cuba.

You can find details at the end of this book.

1

BENNY HILL'S IMMIGRATION CONTROL

Failed at the first hurdle. Destined never to enter Cuba, and all because I decided the most important Spanish phrase to learn was *dos cerveza, por favor*.

The border control officer in the Havana airport eyed me suspiciously while my girlfriend, Sally, stared at me with her *what the hell is happening* look. This holiday was supposed to make us, and it seemed it had broken us before we'd even got into the country.

Then Sally rolled her eyes and shook her head.

I'm doomed. We're doomed. The whole world is doomed.

The officer repeated what she'd said. Not understanding, I showed her our passports. Again. She shook her head. Again. Stalemate.

Her hair belonged in the eighties, her make-up in the seventies, and her uniform in the sixties. If I'd concentrated on listening to her and not working out what parts of her had come from what decade, I might have understood.

She frowned and said the sentence for the third time.

I tried unsuccessfully to pull my lips over my crooked teeth into a smile. Sweat ran from my salt-and-pepper hair down my face, and I felt a single bead of moisture on the tip of my beaked nose. The heat was wreaking havoc on my system, which was accustomed to the UK's ever-changing and much-cooler weather. My being a pound or two stone overweight didn't help matters.

I shrugged, held up my hands, and shook my head. The pressure was increasing, as were my anxiety levels. My fears about coming to Cuba were being realised already.

"Kevin, what's going on?" Sally said, waving her arms around, her face contorted. "Why are we stuck here? There are loads of people behind us. Can't we go through?" Suddenly, she clutched at her chest and took sharp, shallow breaths. I wanted to collapse on the floor in a heap and hope it would all be sorted out in my absence.

Instead, I said, "Everything is fine. You'll be okay. I promise you." I put a soothing hand on her shoulder, which she shrugged off. "She doesn't speak English," I said, nodding towards the officer. "A language barrier, but I'll solve the problem." I had no clue how to solve the problem.

"Darling, I can't breathe." She held the back of her hand to her head and her legs wobbled.

I grabbed her around the waist. "Okay. You're having a panic attack. Now close your eyes and focus on your breathing." Her knees buckled. I held her tighter. "Whoa there. Now breathe in one, two, three, four, five, and out; one, two, three, four, five. Great. Now carry on."

Meanwhile, my breathing had become shallow. My heart pumped furiously. My nerves were shattered. In my head, I went through my priorities. *First, sort out the love of my life. Next, figure out what the officer is saying. Finally, if I haven't keeled over, fix my breathing and my racing heart.*

The border control officer repeated herself yet again. I held out my hands. "One minute, please." I heard a murmur in the queue. Unrest was building.

Ouch!

I glanced down and saw a toy fire truck by my foot, where

it had landed after banging against my ankle. I looked up at the queue to see a grinning toddler in a pushchair. "Hey, little fellow, I think this is yours." I patted him on the head and smiled, thankful for the momentary distraction. My breathing deepened, and my heart rate slowed a little.

"Josh, what have I told you about throwing your toys at people?" the boy's stressed-out mum said. "I'm so sorry."

"It's fine, he's playing. I'm not hurt." I hobbled a step forward to manoeuvre myself out of range of the missile-launching youngster then checked on Sally, who appeared to be breathing normally. She took out her phone. Excellent. She was on the mend. Now to work out what the hell I needed to do. I twirled round to my new nemesis.

"There's no signal! Why's there no internet?"

I sighed internally and pirouetted back to Sally. My resentment at her incessant and increasing demands was growing second by second. We were here in Cuba to fix our rocky relationship. Go on an adventure, win the girl, and live happily ever after. Seemed the joke was on me.

"One minute," I said calmly. "I need to deal with this first."

Her face fell. "I thought you were a big-shot manager. Surely you can sort this out." I'd never claimed that mantle. More accurately, I was middle management at a housing association, where I worked with residents. I loved the job and the people but was far from a high-powered boss. I'd never been fixated on status. I couldn't say the same for my girlfriend.

"I will. Just give me time." I turned around, stepped towards the booth, and shrugged again at the official, who shook her dark, permed hair as though she were a model in an advertisement for shampoo and then stuck her finger out. I followed it to a sign taped on the window of her booth.

Aha, the tourist card. After all that. I took a deep breath as relief pulsed through me.

Even before the trip, the bureaucracy had loomed large.

To visit Cuba, you couldn't simply fill in a form with a stubby blue pen on the plane and hand it in at border control. I'd applied beforehand, and the visa was good for only thirty days and one visit. Details needed included name, address, photo, shoe size, passport number, flight numbers, addresses of where we were staying, and inside leg measurement.

I turned towards Sally, who was still engrossed in her phone. "Babe, have you got the tourist cards?"

Her gaze shot up and her eyes widened. "What? No. You said you'd deal with all the paperwork. Have you lost them? Are they throwing us out?"

"Hang on, wait"—I picked up my bag— "a minute." I buried my head and hands in it, saw an envelope that looked right, picked it up, and held it towards the light. "Aha. Got them." I turned to Sally, grinning.

"Don't do that to me," she said with a snarl. "You're stressing me out. You never think about me, always all about poor Kevin."

My grin slid into a grimace. I turned to the booth and handed the tourist cards over.

The official gave them a cursory glance, stamped them, and nodded us through, waving to the people next in line.

"About bloody time," someone behind me muttered.

Cheeky so-and-so. I kept my head down and ushered Sally through. "Right, let's go," I said, trying to muster cheerfulness into my voice.

Sally took a few steps and halted. "Babe, still no internet. I need to check my messages."

I stared at the mobile in her hand. "Why? We're in Cuba. We don't need our phones here."

This time Sally grimaced. "Don't be a smart arse. I want to see how Harry is."

I gave her my confused look—a very natural look for me. "But he hasn't got a phone."

"God, you're so annoying. What if something has happened and his dad needs to contact me?"

My legs were heavy. I was exhausted already. "Okay," I said with a sigh. "You're right, I'm just . . . I don't know. I think there's Wi-Fi at the hotel."

Sally stomped off in front of me, leaving me to pick up both backpacks and trundle after her. How was this my fault?

On the other side of border control, I wondered for a moment if we'd passed through a portal into a Benny Hill sketch. All the female staff in the border control area wore khaki uniforms that included miniskirts and patterned stockings. The only thing missing was the speeded-up music of a silent film to signify a chase.

I got my phone out.

"What are you doing?" Sally hissed.

"I'm taking a photo. Why?"

"Don't be a dick, Kevin."

I looked at her incredulously.

"Put that thing away. I expressly forbid you to take any photos. You don't want to look like a perv—I don't want you getting arrested as soon as we set foot in Cuba. God, you're a grown man in your forties, not a pubescent teenager."

As she spoke, her eyes rolled. I couldn't work out whether this was an after-effect of the panic attack or a result of my grating on her nerves. Either way, I didn't want to argue. And anyway, she had a point. I couldn't remember if it was illegal to take photos in the border control area. Some countries could be a little funny about photos being taken of their security staff, and we were in a communist country—these weren't exactly known for their tolerance. I slid the phone back in my pocket and tried to hide my disappointment. "You're right. Sorry."

I was lucky to have her in my life. She took care of me. And she was my last chance at love.

We'd met on a dating app, and I was immediately

attracted to her playfulness and physical beauty. It didn't take me long to ask her out, and when she said yes, I was gobsmacked. I'd been convinced she'd laugh in my face.

On our first date, we quickly established shared interests, including house music, raves, and travel. Unfortunately, she didn't share my love for Star Wars—my joke about my being the Han to her Leia fell flat. The more I got to know her, the more I sensed that underneath her sometimes cold and hard exterior was a softer side, and I made it my mission to melt her heart. She told me in the early days that what she loved about me was my kind and tender heart. No one had ever said that about me before. I was the one whose heart melted.

Now, almost two years later, here we were, on an adventure in Cuba.

Sally shuffled behind me like a petulant teenager. I hoped my amazing surprise would cheer her up. "Why are we waiting here?" she asked when I stopped in the arrivals area.

"You'll find out soon enough."

"I hate surprises." She wiped her brow and dropped her hand heavily against her side.

A bubbly, tingly feeling travelled from my belly to my hands, making them shake. Excitement? More likely nerves, I decided. An affliction that had become more prevalent in recent months, as our relationship had descended into a cycle of break-ups and make-ups. "But this one is fabulous."

"I don't like them full stop."

I blew air out of my lungs as my tummy bubbled away. "Be patient. I'm looking for something." I scanned the foyer like a killer robot trying to lock onto my target.

"Well." She placed a hand on her hip. "What are we waiting for?"

"Soon, darling. I promise." I bit on my thumbnail and turned my head away from Sally.

"I can see what you're doing, chewing on your nail like a baby." She hated when I bit my nails and had unleashed all manner of threats and admonishments to get me to stop, including withdrawal of intimacy. At one point she painted my nails with a lacquer that she told me would make me physically sick if I tried to chew them. It worked until I learned to lick it off. Despite its peppery taste, no after-effects followed.

Damn her eagled-eye vision.

I looked again but still couldn't spot somebody holding a sign with Sally's name on it.

She stamped her foot. "Right, I'm tired and I want to go to our hotel. You're starting to get on my bloody nerves."

Starting to?

I caved. "Okay, I booked us a Cadillac. One of those classic American cars from the 1950s."

"Aw, so lovely, darling." She smiled, but my victory was short-lived—it left her face like a thief in the night. "Where is it?"

"Not sure. I asked for someone to be here, waiting for us, with a sign with your name on it. I wanted it to be a treat for you." I peered around, desperately now.

"So thoughtful, darling. Where's the car?"

"I don't know." If I were a killer robot, they would have decommissioned me at this point.

She cocked her head. "Are you sure you made a booking?"

Yes. I rummaged in my pocket and pulled out a piece of paper. After checking it, I held it towards her. "Yeah, here's the confirmation."

Sally snatched it and glanced over its contents. "Where's the car?" she asked again, unhelpfully.

"I don't understand. I arranged for the car online."

Sally had made it clear there was no Wi-Fi, so I couldn't email the company. A sense of dread washed over me.

Looking on the verge of collapse, Sally slouched. "I'm tired. Let's go." While sympathetic—it had been a long day, after all: sixteen-odd hours of travelling, including a three-hour stopover in Madrid—I also resented her attitude. Sometimes it felt as though whatever I did would never be good enough. And her contribution to the trip so far, in terms of both finances and effort, had been minimal. I'd done all the research, made all the bookings, and with no thanks. Feeling my anger rising, I told myself to focus on something positive.

She stopped asking where the car is, I thought. *That's something.*

"Where's my Cadillac?"

I exhaled slowly. Not willing to concede defeat just yet, I decided to do something that no British man wants to do, ever: go to the information desk and ask for help. The shame. The embarrassment. I hung my head momentarily.

The surly woman in the booth grew surlier as I approached. Was she pouting?

"Hi, can you help me, please?" I asked, without much hope, placing my email confirmation on the desk.

She said something in Spanish. I shrugged and shook my head. She repeated my gesture back to me. I picked up the paper, turned around, looked up, and let out an enormous sigh.

"Are you okay?"

My head jolted downwards at the sound of a friendly and sympathetic voice. Before me stood the stressed-out mum from earlier. Josh had the engine in his hand, ready to launch. I moved to the side, placing his mum between us. "I ordered a classic car to take us to the hotel," I explained, "but it's not turned up and I don't understand why."

"Oh dear," she said, pursing her lips. "I'm so sorry to hear that. Happens all the time here."

"What does?"

"Well, people ordering and paying for a classic car which never turns up, and they lose the money." She tilted her head and half-smiled at me.

My heart sunk. "Seriously?"

"Do you have your booking form?"

I handed it to her. She studied it and nodded. "Okay, yeah, right. So, this number here?" She frowned slightly. "Not a Cuban number. I'm afraid you've lost your money."

She handed the sheet back to me. I stared at it and vigorously shook my head. "I'm sure that can't be the case. I don't fall for scams . . ."

She touched my arm. "I'm so sorry, believe me, easily done. Sometimes the problem can be right before our eyes, if only we want to spot it."

I glanced at Sally, who was standing several feet away and scowled. "Thank you for your help," I said to the woman, before heading back to Sally, who now had both her hands on her hips.

"What were you talking to that woman about? What was so interesting about her?"

I stared at the confirmation email, still in disbelief. "Oh, nothing. She tried to help me, I guess."

"I worry about you sometimes, chatting to other women. I don't trust you when you do that."

My head jerked up. Not this again. "You talk to other men."

"That's different. I'm just playing and being flirtatious. You're being, well, I'm not sure what, but stop it. You're with me, remember?" She poked a finger in my chest, and I stepped back.

"You can trust me, Sally. I've never betrayed you and I never will." I placed my hands on her arms and stared at her earnestly. The emotional agony of being cheated on by one of my exes still seared my heart. Even though it had been several years since we broke up, I was still in the process of healing. I couldn't fathom putting anyone through this type of pain.

"Time will tell. Anyway, where's my car?"

2

B-R-E-A-K-U-P

Six months earlier, I was sitting on the sofa in the front room of Sally's house with Harry, her nine-year-old son. The house was in East London, on the border with Essex. The locals feuded over whether they lived in East London or Essex, their arguments dependent on their views of a certain reality TV show.

"Disappear," I said.

No, really, disappear. One hour and thirty minutes with no breaks. Harry had a laser-like focus on improving his spelling skills. I contemplated stopping, but Sally had asked me to help her little angel, and my doing so would pave the way for me to spend the weekend with her. This had become the norm in the relationship. Carrot and stick. Reward and punishment.

I'd tried at the beginning of the relationship—following a disastrous first trip away together, to Margate—to be more me, to stand up for myself. But bit by bit, Sally had, through a battle of wills and what sometimes felt like a war of attrition, whittled away at me.

"D-I-S-A-P-P-E-A-R. Disappear." Harry grinned from ear to ear.

I smiled at him. "Well done. Shall we take a break? I think I need to pee."

"Mummy!" he shouted. "Kevin said a rude word." He turned to me again. "Just a few more spellings, please. Please, Kevin." He made these cow eyes at me, all huge and sad and pleading. His knowledge of my weak spots was disarming. Had he inherited that from his mummy? Hmm.

Children themselves were one of my weak spots. I'd always loved their minds, the way they thought. Harry reminded me of my oldest son, who'd been around Harry's age when I separated from my sons' mum. I sometimes wondered if I overcompensated with Harry, to assuage my guilt for not being a better dad when my two sons were younger. When I left their mum, I felt as if I left them too, and let them down. It would always be my biggest regret.

"No, I didn't!" I shouted at Sally, who was in the conservatory. I turned back to Harry, who clasped his hands and blinked slowly at me. "Okay," I said. "Five more."

Sally appeared in the doorway. "No more. Come on, Harry, Kevin has been doing that for ages now. It's my turn for Kevin's time." She made her own cow eyes at me then spun around and disappeared.

Saved by Sally, and not for the first time.

"One more," Harry said, with a finger to his lips. "Do it quietly."

"Perhaps." As in, perhaps I would, but actually, I wouldn't.

"P-E-R-H-A-P-S. Perhaps." He nodded and waited patiently for his next word.

Had to give it to him—persistent and smart. I needed to choose my next words incredibly carefully.

"Go on, Kevin, do it. PLEASE."

"No." I stood up, and he grabbed me around my knees.

"Easy. N-O. No."

I took short steps as he clung on like the proverbial limpet.

"One more."

I picked him up and placed him gently down while shaking my head and making a point of keeping my lips closed. Walking towards the conservatory, I could see Sally inspecting the walls and ceiling.

"Kevin, come here. I want to show you something."

I turned around, smirked at Harry, stuck my tongue out, and walked away.

As she stared at the ceiling, I drank her in. Always so beautiful. Her shoulder-length dirty-blonde hair cascaded over her shoulders. She turned and smiled at me with her full lips, and her green eyes sparkled in the light. Her pretty face never failed to melt my insides into mushy goo. She was eight years younger than I was and looked even younger than that, blessed by flawless skin.

I wrapped my arm around her shoulders and buried my head in her freshly shampooed hair. At five foot three, she was about four inches shorter than I was. I liked it that way. I was shorter than both my sons, one late teen, the other, early twenties, who relished calling me "Shorty".

Not for the first time, I metaphorically pinched myself. How had I got so lucky to have Sally as my girlfriend? Her decisiveness masked my dithering. The softness beneath her armour was a joy to catch and bring out to the light. The care she showed me regarding my appearance and health reassured me that someone was looking after me better than I looked after myself. Plus, unlike me, she was a real hot-shot manager, in business development in banking.

"You okay?" I said, releasing her.

"Not sure." She glanced at the ceiling again then looked at me. "Babe, you need to be firmer with Harry. He runs rings around you. You're too soft."

"I thought you wanted me to do his spellings with him?" I reached out to her again, but she moved away slightly.

"I do. You have more patience than me, and he loves you, but be the adult and don't let him walk all over you. Not a great look, darling." She studied me for a second then turned away.

"Okay, you're right. Anyway, what's up?" My legs wobbled imperceptibly on the spot. Once again, Sally's words had thrown me. Anxiety had been my baseline emotion in our relationship for the last several months. A chilly autumn had followed an intimate summer.

She pointed at the wooden ceiling. "I think the conservatory needs painting. It'll need doing properly though—rubbing down with sandpaper, sugar soap, then an undercoat and two coats of paint afterwards."

"Hmm, I see." I stroked my chin and tried to look like a tradesperson despite my trade skills being virtually non-existent. Painting I could manage if I took my time, but then again, couldn't everyone? "Massive job. Won't be cheap. Probably take two weekends."

She spun around, her face like thunder. "Well, if you can't, or won't, I'll get Andy to do it." She stood at her full height, throwing her shoulders back. The hint of a smile emerged on her lips.

My hackles rose immediately. Sally's friend. Andy was in love with her, and she often used him as a bargaining chip in our relationship to get her way.

I paused.

Before I could say another word, Sally had her phone out and was tapping away on it. Then she theatrically swiped the screen. "Done. I'm sure Andy will do it. He never says no to me." Panicked, I stood motionless, while my brain contemplated what was happening. His name stabbed me in my heart. Not a threat but, somehow, a man I'd never met felt threatening. My mouth moved, but no words left it. Moments later, her mobile pinged. She smiled at the screen and peeked up at me. "See, I told you he would. He's coming around soon. Which means, darling, you must leave. You know how he feels about you."

I didn't know how he felt. I'd never met the guy. She'd shown me two pictures of him. I got the impression he'd been punched in the face a few times. That didn't stop the jealousy. I hadn't always been a jealous person, but after Dawn, an ex-girlfriend who betrayed me, by cheating on me, the feeling had started worming its way into my psyche. And in recent weeks, it had become a central emotion in my relationship with Sally. I hated the man it made me become. It was a toxin that invaded my body, pushing out the healthy parts and leaving the nasty bits behind. At the same time, I felt helpless to prevent it. Dawn was after my divorce, but several years before I met Sally. Pressure built behind my solar plexus. I curled my hands into fists.

"So, when am I going to meet him? He needs to know about us."

"You've met some of my other friends," Sally said defensively. "And I've not connected with any of yours."

To be fair, I didn't have loads of friends, and when I did meet up with the few I had, it was without partners.

"Okay, let's arrange something."

Sally took two deep breaths, closed her eyes, then reopened them. "I don't like pressure," she said, gripping her face. "This is too much. You're suffocating me. I think you should leave now. I need some space." She walked around me towards the living room.

My throat dried up. "Oh, babe," I croaked, following her. "Don't be like that. I'm sorry, I'll do whatever you want. What do you want?" I reached out and grabbed her arm, but she shook it free.

"You . . . aargh . . . Kevin. I can do without this. I want my relationships to be easy, fun—not stressful. This, between us, doesn't feel like that anymore." She walked to the stairs by the front door and pointed to the exit. "I think you should go."

What? I almost choked on my surprise. How had things

escalated so quickly? Then I thought of our frequent internecine wars of words, on subjects ranging from my dishwasher-stacking skills to my attentiveness as a boyfriend, her lack of desire to meet up as often, and the pressure she said I piled onto her about the relationship. While my desire to meet up also lessened, the compulsion to meet up strengthened. My feelings, of her slipping away, compelled me to act to stop her.

Even so, I felt blindsided. I went to take Sally's hand, but she moved backwards, up three of the stairs.

"Just go. NOW." She covered her face with her hands.

Messed up again. How could I be such an idiot? I took one last look at Sally, who was still holding her face in her hands, before opening the door and slamming it behind me.

One month after the bust up with Sally—which I considered either a permanent split or a temporary separation, depending on my mood and level of optimism in any given moment—I stood at the French doors of my fourth-floor flat chewing on my nails and watching the rain form little puddles on my Juliet balcony. The too-narrow balcony was as useful as a chocolate teapot.

I looked out at the derelict crane straight ahead in the river, a remnant of a wharf that had existed way before they built my block of flats. Parakeets squawked and landed on top of it. Yes really, feral parakeets in London, hard to believe, but true; look it up. Supposedly, I lived the dream: a riverside flat, and a successful career and life in London. But it was all for nothing without Sally.

Turning away from the window, I looked past my living room at the open-plan kitchen. The dishes were piled high in the sink; I ignored them for the thousandth time and shuffled to the sofa, where I stared at my phone for several minutes, willing a message from Sally to arrive. Then I grabbed the unopened bills beside me and placed them on the growing pile on the dusty glass coffee table.

My flat wasn't usually so untidy and grimy. While not the neatest and cleanest forty-something male, normally I was more fastidious. Now, my every waking moment was consumed with thoughts of the break-up and how to win Sally back. Nothing could snap me out of my low mood.

Picking up my mobile again, I opened my messages app. Nothing. No contact from Sally for three weeks now. Usually, contact would occur after a week or so, followed by a meet-up, a make-up, and a honeymoon period of about a month or two before the cycle started again.

Why had this happened? Why had she broken up with me again? The twin harbingers of death of self, rejection and a feeling of inadequacy—had gnawed my insides into nothingness. We'd gone through six break-ups now, and Sally had instigated each one, for various reasons. Once, she said she didn't love me anymore, but a couple of weeks later she changed her mind. Another time, she had a massive argument with her neighbour and then spotted me talking to him later that weekend. She said I'd disrespected and undermined her. I grovelled after that one, as I felt she had a point. I sometimes wondered whether her breaking up with me was her way of testing me. Maybe she wanted to force me to chase her and reassure her I still wanted her. And I did. Despite the confusion and hurt, I still chased after her and wanted her. Why?

Maybe this time it's for real, I thought. *Maybe I'll never hear from her again. Maybe this is the end.* This sent me spiralling into fear. Nothing scared me more than the thought of being alone forever. With no one to talk to, I wouldn't make it in this big, scary world. Who'd take care of me when I was sick? Who'd comfort me?

Why did I pause? Why did I let my jealousy of Andy get the better of me? I thought about Sally being with someone else then smacked the side of my head to rid myself of the image.

My love for her was all-consuming. There was no room for me. Was this how love was supposed to go? Surely. This push-and-pull dynamic was passion. Break-ups and make-ups happened all the time, in every relationship, right?

Since Sally had blocked my number—again—I had no way to contact her, except, perhaps . . . *How about I email her?* That could work. I composed an email expressing my remorse and how much I missed her and wanted us to get back together. Then I pressed send and stared at my phone.

Minutes went by.

I refreshed my phone.

After thirty minutes, I panicked. Maybe my email was broken? I sent myself an email to check. Nothing. *Must be my email. I need to fix it.*

My phone pinged. My heart skipped a beat. Sally?

No, the message I'd sent myself. Damn it.

After an hour, I read the email I'd sent. It was the best email ever. A brilliant and well-written message.

My phone pinged. Sally?

No, a message from my mate Sean. One from my mate Paddy arrived soon after. Both asking how I was. Clearly colluding to check up on me. I didn't have the energy to reply.

I reread my email. God, such an awful message. No wonder she hadn't replied.

I contemplated jumping in my car and driving round to hers, but then what? What if she rejected me again, in person? I gulped and leant forward, trying to catch my breath. No, I couldn't do that. Plus, it was a little stalkery. That wasn't me.

I knew I should message my friends back. We could meet, I could talk about it with them. But I'd been a rubbish friend and didn't feel I could face them. Letting down friends had become a habit lately: missed birthdays, significant events, meals—always because I was with Sally, or doing something for her, or trying to win her back.

I felt genuine happiness almost exclusively when I was

with Sally or my family. But whenever I said goodbye to my parents and sons, particularly my sons, after spending time with them, sadness overwhelmed me. In moments of reflection, I could see that deep down, I'd never believed I'd been good enough as a father, or a son.

And the happiness with Sally was punctuated by periods of depression. I didn't deal well with the emptiness inside me. My coping mechanisms involved throwing myself into work and alcohol. Drinking was a constant in my life. When I wasn't with Sally, the void inside me grew even bigger and gnawed away at me, until we were together again.

Regardless of my relationship status, the void was always there in some form. I had no real sense of myself and what I wanted from (and to contribute to life). Purpose and peace had always eluded me, and I didn't know why. What I did know was that matters had deteriorated following my acrimonious split from Dawn. And no one could help me with that. Not even Sally.

Two hours later, my phone pinged. I jumped. My hands shook as I opened my email. This time, there was a message from Sally.

She wanted to meet.

Oh, joy of joys, we were getting back together! At last.

I fist-bumped the air, adrenaline pumping through my body. All my self-doubt melted away like mist on a summer's morning.

3

COCKROACH JIG

"Well, what's happening?" Sally said, poking a finger towards me. "I want my classic car, and I want to go to our hotel."

Whatever I told her would disappoint her. Each second I stood still, the bags—two backpacks and two shoulder bags—weighed heavier. I wondered whether I'd eventually just collapse. That might be the best option.

My brain whirred, making the computations. The classic car wasn't happening. I'd been scammed. I'd process that later. Right now, I had to be decisive. "Let's find a taxi. But before that, we need some currency."

"Why? I thought you said you were getting some money before we flew out?"

I viewed Sally, collecting my patience. "I couldn't. You can't get it back home."

"Why?"

Purchasing Cuban dollars was impossible in the UK, although there's probably some dodgy bloke in a market somewhere in London who'll sell you some—and God only knows if it'd be the real deal, and at what exchange rate.

I'd done quite a bit of research beforehand, as is my forte, and learned that in Cuba, a socialist country, the money was controlled by the state. That way, they stopped money from being traded privately and could keep a tight hand on the rate. I knew all that and I could have said all that. Instead, exhausted, I said, "You can't. I have to find an exchange booth here."

I braced myself for another argument, but she just gave me a look that said *get on with it*, so I led the way out of the airport. As we exited the arrivals foyer, a blast of humid air hit me. Within nanoseconds, my upper body was soaked.

I scanned left and right and spotted the currency bureau to the right. "This way, Sally."

Reaching the bureau, I dumped the bags and stretched, the relief from the weight immediate. The rate was 1.5 Cuban convertible pesos to 1 English pound, the same as the US dollar to the English pound. I assumed the Cuban government wanted their money to be worth the same as the imperialist Yankee dollar. The currency booth exchanged pounds, euros, and Canadian dollars, but for US-dollar exchange, they slapped on an additional 10 per cent fee. Was this because of US sanctions, which made it more expensive? In other words, was it a genuine cost to be recouped? Or was it a retaliatory effort for the way they'd been treated? Either way, I admired the small country for standing up to a much larger one. No one likes a bully.

I changed up two hundred pounds or quid as we say in the UK to see us through the first few days. "Here we go," I said, stepping towards Sally, who stood tapping her foot, arms folded. "We have money. Now to find a taxi."

"This was a bad idea. You. This holiday. Everything."

Geez. We hadn't even properly got out of the airport yet. I felt myself deflate. Despite all my efforts, this was her response. My mouth opened, but no words came out.

She stared at me contemptuously. "Can we go now? I want to get to the hotel—NOW!" Classic travel-day Sally. Anxious, impatient, and rude. At least, I hoped it was just travel-day Sally and not the lead-up to yet another break-up.

I spotted a line of yellow taxis up ahead. "Over there," I said, nodding towards them. "Let's jump in one of them."

She glanced over. "I want a better one than that. I want my Cadillac."

I inhaled sharply. "I don't know where they are and you said you wanted to leave," I said firmly, "so let's grab one of them. It'll be quicker."

"Okay." She strode ahead, leaving her bags with me. Again.

"I'll carry yours as well, shall I?"

She twirled around. "What? What was that?"

"Yeah, you stand in the queue and I'll bring the bags."

"Okay." She continued her striding.

"I'll fetch both backpacks because now I'm your personal porter," I muttered.

"What's that?"

Damn Sally and her bat-like hearing.

"Coming, baby."

Fortunately, there was no queue for the taxis. We were met by a suave-looking man wearing a Panama hat and shaded sunglasses, which seemed superfluous, given that it was evening. I hated when people wore shades at night. In my youth, some people wore them in nightclubs. Idiots. Yes, I was one of them.

I showed the driver my email confirmation from the hotel and pointed to the address. He smiled, nodded, and went round the back of his cab and opened the boot. "Please, your bags."

"You speak English then?" I asked as I got into the front seat. A stupid question.

"Yes, for us drivers it helps. Plus, I am an educated man, so I learn more than one language."

As we made our way from the airport, the absence of light, people, and cars struck me. There were no commercial centres on the outskirts of Havana. We had the road to ourselves except for the occasional packed bus. It was surreal to me. In London, the time of day had little effect on the volume of people and traffic.

Smells wafted in through the driver's window, the only available air conditioning: something exotically sweet one minute and sewage the next. Now and again, the taxi would slow down and zigzag around potholes and the occasional small crater. Luckily, the driver had an encyclopaedic knowledge of every crevice and canyon on the road—he avoided every single one.

I turned left towards the driver. It was an odd sensation. In the UK, the driver sits on the right. "So, you said you're an educated man," I said, breaking the comfortable silence.

"Of course. Taxi drivers in Havana, we are very well educated." He gesticulated with his right hand but kept his left hand firmly on the steering wheel. "I used to be a doctor, but now I drive taxis."

"Why?"

He shrugged. "Because I am better paid as a driver."

What? I turned my full attention to him. "How is that possible?"

"As a doctor, I was paid in pesos," he said, overtaking a slow-moving bus. "Now I earn bucks. Everybody wants tourist currency. Worth many times more than the peso. Now I'm well off and can buy what my family needs."

"So, doctors in Cuba don't earn a good income?"

"If you work for the government, in health, no. You're poorly paid. But in taxis, there's much better income."

"Really?" I said incredulously.

He shrugged again. "Yes."

This was the kind of conversation I wanted while I was here. I was eager to talk to the locals and find out what they thought about communism, Cuba, and Che.

I turned towards the back seat, wondering if Sally had been listening to the conversation. But she was staring at her mobile and seemed miserable. I sighed and thought again about how I could cheer her up. Should we go out on the town? Did they even have one to go out on? I knew the hotel had Wi-Fi, so we could have a couple of drinks there and she could read those messages she was so keen to see.

Looking back out of my window, I couldn't believe how dark Havana was. The only light I saw came from the small number of homes we passed, and even that was usually just the glare of a TV screen.

Then I spotted the sea. A shiver of excitement ran through me. I knew our hotel overlooked the water. We had to be getting close. "Where are we now?"

"This is the world-famous Malecón," the driver said proudly.

I'd read about Havana's famous promenade. There were more lights now, and I saw locals walking around, many of them families with small children. I also saw fishermen and what appeared to be prostitutes.

Thirty-five minutes after leaving the airport, we passed under an archway and into a long palm-tree-lined driveway. The hotel's exterior was impressive. The extensive white building with bell towers on either side was set on a small hill and had several floors. Our driver hauled our bags out of his boot and onto the pavement, and a hotel employee grabbed them and took them inside. I shook the driver's hand and wished him well, grateful for my first conversation with a local. I'd already learned that the economy here was structured much differently than I was used to. I was looking forward to exploring this further.

In the lobby, Sally and I were greeted by colonial

grandeur. It was stamped into every nook and cranny. The broad lobby extended the entire width of the hotel and was punctuated by various booths and I guessed a bar or restaurant or two. The place had a 1930s Art Deco feel, with dark wooden beams, yellow-painted archways, mosaic walls, and a tiled wooden floor. Grandfather clocks appeared sporadically, and small Roman columns held baskets containing cacti. Hanging lights and chandeliers lit the space.

This prestigious hotel was a luxurious beginning to our holiday yet Sally still looked miserable as she gazed around. My brain worked overtime on solutions. What would make her happy? What could I do to brighten her mood?

The history of the hotel? I had to admit I loved how the building was steeped in the past.

"Right then," I said, turning to her. "Back in the day, before the revolution, Havana was a popular holiday destination for Americans, like the Costa del Sol for us Brits. It was favoured by the Mafia before Castro stopped all that and imposed communism on the country."

"Uh-huh."

"He nationalised the hotel following the revolution."

Sally yawned. I took that as my cue to shut up. She used to love my encyclopaedic knowledge of useless facts. Less so recently.

Check-in involved an attendant looking at the piece of paper with my booking confirmation, looking at Sally and me, looking at an antiquated computer screen—one of those huge ones from the 1990s, longer than it was wide—banging on the keyboard and looking again at the sheet of paper I'd handed her. Meanwhile, I panicked. Was there a problem with my booking? Did I do something wrong? Memories of Margate flooded me.

Eventually, she took our passports and made copies, and I breathed a sigh of relief.

We were escorted to our rooms by a porter, our bags carried for us. Another relief. My shoulders couldn't take much more. Outside our room, I tipped the man and checked out the plaque on the wall. Turned out we were staying in the Rita Hayworth Room. According to the plaque, she'd had her honeymoon in our room. It didn't specify which one, though. I'd hoped for the Orson Welles Room—a bit of gravitas and a smattering of intellectualism. Or perhaps the Winston Churchill Room or the Ernest Hemingway Room.

But I pointed at the plaque and said cheerfully, "Look, darling, we're staying in the Rita Hayworth Room."

"Oh, really?" Sally leaned in to get a better view. "Wow, I love Rita Hayworth."

"Yeah, she had one of her honeymoons here. I think she was married more times than you."

"Har-har."

Sally had been hitched three times and had even hinted at marriage number four during our better periods. I often teased her about how many times she'd been married, but she never enjoyed the joke and I never took the hint.

Marriage didn't suit me. Experience had shown me that. Nothing to do with commitment issues—I loved being in a long-term relationship. But the practicalities of divorce provided an ample battleground for the parties to wage war and weaponise their pain. And I'd never met a poor divorce lawyer.

This was our relationship now. I'd crack jokes about her three marriages and Sally would "har-har" sarcastically. Almost two years together will do that to you. "How about we dump our bags and head down to the bar and grab a couple of mojitos on the terrace?"

"Great idea," she said. "One of your better ones."

"Har-har."

∽

In the terrace bar, our chairs facing outwards towards the sea, I took a deep breath and grinned. "Wow, we made it. Here we are, drinking mojitos in Havana."

A handful of the tables scattered about were occupied. Gardens flanked the terrace, and a palm-tree-lined path led to the water. In the distance, a peacock and peahen meandered in the grass, taking a romantic evening stroll. Closer, tall white flowers swayed in the gentle breeze.

"Yeah, we did," Sally said. "Can't quite believe it myself." She gave me a small smile before looking back down at her phone.

An understatement. I was shocked we'd made it this far—both to Cuba and as a couple. A few times, during our more uncertain periods, I'd contemplated coming to Cuba on my own. But each time, I'd quickly dismiss the idea. It terrified me, the thought of travelling on my own. There was so much that could go wrong. Nothing was scarier to me than feeling utterly vulnerable. That and the thought of dying, of course. Dying on my own, now that would be the perfect storm.

Sally furrowed her brow. "Is your Wi-Fi working, darling?"

"Not sure, not checked yet." I gazed out at the sea. "Gorgeous, heh?"

"Can you check? Mine keeps cutting in and out." She banged her finger on the screen and tossed the phone onto the table.

"Don't worry," I said on an exhale. "We're in Cuba. Who needs the internet when we have Cuba?"

"Cuba is all well and good, but I need to make sure Harry is okay." She picked up her phone again and studied it.

"He'll be fine," I said, waving a hand dismissively. "He's with his dad. He'll be having a whale of a time staying up late, eating rubbish, and watching crap on television."

Sally stared at me, shaking her head. "Typical of you.

Everything's a joke, isn't it. This is my son, my flesh and blood, we're talking about. I need to know he's okay."

All I wanted was to relax. Why couldn't she chill the hell out? I swallowed my annoyance. "I'm sorry, I was titting about. I'll check."

She crossed her legs and turned her body slightly away from mine. I could see I wouldn't get a moment's peace on this holiday, catering to her every need. But it would all be worth it, making her happy and securing our happily ever after.

I pulled my phone out of my jeans and checked the Wi-Fi signal. "Here we go. Yes, I've got two bars, I think. But I've had no internet since we landed."

Sally gawped at her screen. "Only got one bar, and that keeps disappearing."

"No worries, we can use my mobile for messages if you need to contact Harry," I said, placing a soothing hand on her arm. "We'll sort it out."

She looked up and stuck her face close to mine. "I want to contact MY son, on MY phone, in MY own time, and on MY own."

What the hell? I knew her moods could switch quickly, but I couldn't work out why the Wi-Fi issue was upsetting her so much. I cleared my throat. "One more for the road?" I said, in a barely concealed attempt to divert Sally's attention.

"Yes, but I need the Wi-Fi sorting too."

What did she expect me to do? Not my fault the Wi-Fi was rubbish. I stood and headed towards the reception, where I collared a waiter and ordered two more drinks. Then I wandered around the lobby trying to find a hotspot. The signal was as temperamental as Sally, so I asked at reception and was told that outside on the terrace was a good place for the Wi-Fi.

Great. I half-expected Sally to tell me to install better Wi-Fi next.

When I broke the news to Sally, who was still fiddling with her phone, she shook her head and muttered something under her breath. She'd finished her second drink, so I ordered her another one. And another three after that.

When the bill came, I cringed, expecting the worst. But the cocktails worked out to three pounds each. In one of the most luxurious hotels in Havana. The best mojitos in my extensive experience. In London, they would have cost four times that in a regular bar. Maybe this trip wouldn't be a total disaster after all.

Sally was being murdered. It was the only explanation for the screams that forced me to sit bolt upright in bed.

I frantically tried to make out what was happening through blurry vision, as I didn't have my glasses on. Sally appeared to be standing in a corner of the room. The bathroom light was on.

"Wha . . . what . . . what's happened? Are you okay? What's going on?" I scrambled out of bed and towards Sally, who was hyperventilating. Confusion and panic vied for my attention as she threw herself into my arms. "Deep breaths now." I rubbed her back then pulled away and stroked her face.

"Oh my God . . . A cockroach . . . In the bathroom . . . You must find . . . and kill it . . . It's huge . . . I nearly stood on . . . Darling, please don't stand still. Kill it. Hurry, hurry, go on now." She pushed me away.

I staggered a little but maintained my balance. "Remember, big breaths." I imitated breathing deeply.

"Go. NOW." Sally bent forward, arms at shoulder height, shooing me away. I tried to gather my wits. As far as I could work out, there were two key facts: one, there was a cockroach in the bathroom; two, Sally was scared and murderous and wanting me to kill. At least she wasn't being murdered.

"Hurry," she urged, her eyes wide, her eyebrows high. "Kill it before the monster comes in here. I won't be able to sleep otherwise. Murder it! Come on, you're a man, aren't you?"

Oh great, now my "manliness" was being called into question. I took a deep breath, turned around, and walked on tiptoes, trying not to make a sound as I made my way to the bathroom. I wasn't a fan of enormous insects.

That's a lie. They scared the hell out of me.

Within feet of the doorway, I paused to summon my courage.

"KILL IT."

As I flattened my feet on the ground, I puffed out my chest and, with Sally's words of "encouragement" ringing in my ear, slowly peered in. There it crouched, in the middle of the floor. An enormous monster of a creature. Huge and horrible.

I slowly brought my head back out of the doorway, fumbled for the door handle, and pulled the door shut, watching the floor to ensure the insect didn't escape. Then I kicked myself for not researching how to kill a cockroach or whether I faced any danger of being stung or bitten. I remembered seeing films where people had stamped on them. I leant against the wall, catching my breath and contemplating my next move.

"Have you killed it?" Sally said, flailing her arms, still in the same spot in the corner. "What are you doing?"

I put my index finger to my mouth then moved to the bed and eased on my white trainers.

"What the hell are you doing? Oh God, it'll come in here. I know it will. Hurry."

Armed with my killer trainers, I crept back towards the

bathroom. I had no intention of stamping on that thing barefoot. Eurgh, just the thought. I gagged. Standing before the door, I slowly pushed on it and placed my foot in the widening gap. Light escaped but thankfully no cockroach. When the space was wide enough, I slithered in and slammed the door. Gripping the handle, I slowly turned my head. It was still there, in the middle of the floor.

Taking a deep breath, I twisted my whole body around, raised my foot, and launched it forward before bringing it down hard. But the sneaky little bugger scuttled to the side.

"Hey, that's cheating!"

I lifted my foot and stamped down again. Several times. But the errant insect dodged my trainer each time. Then I used both feet, doing a passable impression of an Irish dancer. While I didn't kill the offending creature, my little jig did scare it away, into a hole at the bottom of the bath. At least my lovely white trainers stayed clean. I got a load of tissue paper, blocked the hole, and doubled over as a mixture of breathlessness and adrenaline hit me.

"Did you kill the disgusting insect, darling?" Sally asked from the corner, as I climbed back into bed. "I won't sleep tonight."

"It got away."

"Oh, Kevin, go back in and murder it." Now I wasn't only not a "real man"—I was a failure.

"Listen, the insect scarpered under the bath panel, so I blocked off the hole. It won't be able to get back in. You're safe now. I promise."

"Typical. I should have done it myself. Useless." She tiptoed towards the bed.

"It won't be coming back."

"Well, if it does. I'll be stamping on your head." She got into bed, turned her back to me, and within two minutes was snoring.

Meanwhile, I lay on my back, eyes wide open, adrenaline sprinting through my body along with a resounding message: "CREATURE ALERT! STAY AWAKE. DANGER. DANGER!"

What the hell was I doing here?

4
MAKE OR BREAK

A couple of days after receiving Sally's email, I sat at the dining table in her freshly painted conservatory. Andy had clearly followed through on his offer. I searched for signs of poor workmanship, without success.

Moving my attention to Sally, who sat opposite me, I searched for signs of her mood, desperate to work out how this would go. She wouldn't look at me, just stared at the table.

Finally, I broke the silence. "I've missed you."

My nerves were frayed. I hoped this was a reconciliation; I feared it was the end of our relationship. The ultimate rejection.

Have you ever tried leaving your phone alone for more than a few minutes when you have nothing to do? It's the best comparison I have to my relationship with Sally. Even if I'd wanted to, I couldn't leave her alone. I felt compelled to be with her. That lack of control worried me, but not as much as not being with her.

Sally peeked up at me and then paused, seemingly for effect, before saying, "We are over and finished."

I bolted up as a volcano erupted in the pit of my belly. "Wha . . . why . . . I don't understand?"

She sighed, waving her hand in a *sit-down* gesture. "Don't interrupt. Listen for once. For goodness sake, I knew this was a mistake."

"I'm sorry," I said, sitting back down. "Carry on . . . please." I'd always found it difficult reining my emotions in, especially with her.

"I'm bored with our relationship," she said with a sigh. "I want excitement, to travel the world, but you don't." She held out her hand, sensing perhaps I was about to interrupt her. Caught out, I glanced away to hide my embarrassment. "What's the point," she continued. "Unless something drastic changes?"

I shook my head. Now it was my turn to stare at the table, from which I sought inspiration. After our last trip together, to Marrakesh, my travel bug had upped and left. "I'll change. What do you want me to be—I mean do?"

"I don't think you have it in you, to be honest. You say you love me, yet you continue to behave in ways that tell me the opposite."

I wasn't above begging. "I'm sorry. I want to travel, but after what happened in Morocco . . . It's been hard, getting past that. Give me a chance. One last time."

"Maybe." She shrugged. "I don't know."

"What do you want me to do?" I reached across the table to hold her hands, but she sat back in her chair, so I slumped back in mine.

"Harry is with his shit bag of a father this Christmas and I don't want to spend the time in the UK."

I straightened. Was she giving me a chance to redeem myself? "Oh, like a holiday?"

"I want somewhere hot."

"Okay . . ."

"But not any old place. Needs to be better than Margate." She gave me a pointed look. "Somewhere *abroad*. Still can't believe you took me to the seaside to romance me. Do you remember?"

How could I forget?

It was before we'd started dating officially when I was still trying to woo her. Okay, I realise now that taking her to Margate for a romantic getaway wasn't my greatest idea—especially since she'd wanted to go to Barcelona. In my defence, she hadn't said that outright, only hinted. Not one of my finest moments, but my heart was in the right place. I was still paying the price; I now had little input regarding any decisions in our relationship.

The TV was on in the background. Barack Obama, the American president, was announcing loosening restrictions on travel to Cuba and ushering in a new era of relations.

"Yeah," I said, "but I also took you to Marrakesh." A place way out of my comfort zone.

"Yeah and look what happened. You won't travel abroad now. We haven't been anywhere since."

"I did nearly meet my maker." That wasn't an exaggeration. At least not much. I shuddered. "I need time, that's all."

"Time for what? Grow old, go nowhere, and die?" Sally leant in and grimaced. "Cuba is where I want to go," she said, nodding towards the TV. "That would kick us out of this rut."

I scratched my head and glanced at the TV. "You realise Cuba is a commie country? Why the hell would you want to go there? You hate anything left-wing."

"Do you know anyone else who's gone?" She raised her eyebrows.

I half shook, half nodded my head. "No one. And there are probably excellent reasons for that. Can't be safe. Why would anyone want to go?"

"Because it's different. Because no one else goes there. Because I want adventure."

"This is a worse idea than Marrakesh."

We'd taken the fateful trip to Morocco several months earlier. I'd wanted to stay in or around our hotel with its rooftop pool and bar and relative safety. Sally had more dangerous ideas, like exploring the markets and souks. I favoured the safety and security of resort-style holidays, whereas Sally preferred backpacking and venturing off the beaten track.

It was driving a wedge between us.

"Babe, we're lost," I said, holding up a gigantic map of the souks of Marrakesh, twisting it one way and another. Nothing made sense.

Sally halted a few steps in front of me. "I hope you're joking, darling?" She waltzed over to me, one hand on her hip, her brow furrowed, and her lips pursed.

I turned the map around again before peering up at Sally. "No. I said we should have stayed inside the market, kept to straight lines."

"Oh, my fault then?" she said, placing her hands on her chest. "I told you, you're responsible for directions and keeping us safe. You know I have no sense of direction."

I dropped my hand with the map in it to my side in exasperation. "Yeah, but you wandered off. I told you before that we should have turned back."

"But I want to explore! What's the point of coming to Morocco if we don't visit the souks?" she said, gesturing to our surroundings. Then she stepped right into my space and jabbed her finger into my chest. "So how are you going to get us back to the hotel?"

I stepped sideways and sighed, raising the map again. "I don't know yet. I'm hoping we'll come to a landmark that I can match to the map."

"Why can't you use your phone?"

Not helpful, as always. I'm not an idiot. Okay, not strictly true. "Because, my love, we don't have internet here, and the maps won't work without a connection."

"Well, where are we?" She twirled around.

"I'm trying to figure that out, darling."

"What have I said to you before? Don't come to me with problems—come to me with solutions."

Excellent. Now she thinks I'm one of her staff members. I'm your lover, for God's sake. "A solution is what I'm working on."

"Fine. Quit moaning then. Pull yourself together and stop focusing solely on yourself for a change."

She had to be joking. But I held my tongue and scanned my surroundings then checked the map. "Right, let's go this way." I pointed ahead of me and started walking. I had no clue where "this way" would take us, but I hoped to buy some time and get us the hell away from the small crowd that was gathering. Several locals were pointing at us.

Stranger danger.

My palms grew wet as my face reddened. I thought my heart might just burst out of my chest. Sweat spread from under my arms like a virus. I stopped again. There was a street sign. I turned around to find Sally outside a shop selling metalwork, carpets, spices, lanterns, jewellery, and pottery. Shaking my head, I buried it in the map, trying to find the street name.

"Darling. The lantern. So beautiful."

"Yes, gorgeous."

"Are you even looking?"

I glanced up and saw a lantern that looked like all the lanterns we'd seen earlier.

"How much for this?" she asked the shopkeeper.

He grabbed it and handed it over to her. "For you, madam, special price for only friends. Two hundred and fifty dirhams." He smiled obsequiously.

"Kevin, how much is that? Will you stop looking at that stupid map?" She tried to snatch it out of my hands.

I turned slightly away from her, so she missed, and made a quick mental calculation. "Fifty quid."

"Too much." She tried to return the lantern to the shopkeeper, who shook his hands. "No." She placed it carefully on the ground and walked towards me. I knew the drill. All part of her negotiating strategy.

"Wait. Madam, please. Hold. See. Good. Yes." He ran up to us, lantern in hand, and thrust it under her nose.

I took the lantern and shook my head. "Too much, no." I checked every inch and added, "Sixty dirhams."

"No. Too little. You're trying to buy a plane for the price of a bicycle."

"I think it's the other way round, my friend." I held the lantern towards him.

"Okay, you drive a hard bargain. Two-hundred-dirham, best price." He grinned at us both.

"One-hundred-dirham, last offer," Sally said.

"One hundred. Agreed. You like anything else?"

"Come on, babes," I said. "Buy it and we'll find our way out." I held up the map, ready to try once more to decipher its secrets.

"Excuse me, sir and madam. I show you the way." A short man with stubble and thinning hair stood before us, rubbing his hands. Beside him was a boy of about ten.

"You take us out?" Sally said, enunciating each word. That's how she communicated with foreigners, speaking loudly and slowly so they'd miraculously understand English.

I just shook my head.

"Why yes," he said proudly. "All my life I live here."

My stomach did a cartwheel, and not of excitement. This was a terrible idea. *I got us lost in a foreign country and we're being offered help by two strangers.*

"Aw, thank you." Sally turned to me and smiled. "Aren't they lovely?"

No—they could be serial killers, kidnappers, or worse, rug sellers.

They sauntered away and motioned for us to follow. Sally did so eagerly, and I tagged along. Moments later, I grabbed her hand. "Babe, I've got a bad feeling about this," I said through gritted teeth.

"Don't be silly. You've got us lost. I'm sorting it out. They'll help us. After all, you don't seem to know how to get out." She walked towards them again, and they stopped and urged us forward once more.

When we caught up, they moved swiftly: forward, a sharp right, forward, sharp left, forward, another sharp left, a right, and onwards through narrow alleyways and past shops, homes, and backyards. My head spun. Disorientated, I was convinced the alleyways were getting narrower and that there were fewer people about. We jolted to a halt. Our man and boy argued heatedly with another local, who pointed at us and punched his chest. Were they fighting over us? Was he trying to stop us from being abducted? Should we go with him instead? Our man threw his arms in the air and muttered something that made the other guy recoil. My stomach knotted and my anxiety levels shot skywards.

Then our man turned towards us with a smarmy smile. "Please. Come."

Onwards again. Left, right, forward, right, right, left, forward. The alleyways became even smaller and more claustrophobic. I worried about Sally, who'd been prone to panic attacks recently. But she seemed fine following our guides' lead. I stayed back slightly, wanting to protect her from any surprise attacks. Were we being led to our deaths? To a local warlord? Were we being kidnapped? In catastrophe mode, my mind spewed out every worst-case scenario.

Rug sellers were still a potential outcome.

As we turned into another narrow alley, the man whispered to the boy, and they snooped backwards. Momentarily their gaze fixed on us before they caught themselves and smiled. *Whoa.* My system went from high alert to DEFCON 0. I caught up to Sally and grasped her arm. "Stick with me."

"Oh, you and your 'feelings'," she said, making air quotes and walking ahead a few steps again.

Suddenly, we emerged into one of the major boulevards. Suspicion quickly followed my immense relief. What had I missed?

Sally turned to me. "Darling, give them some money—two pound for their troubles."

The man and boy stuck close to me, the man rubbing his hands with glee. "Thank you," I said, fumbling in the pockets of my shorts. I pulled out my wallet and kept it close to my body. Turning away, I carefully gripped a small note in my sweaty hand. Still holding the wallet close, I tried unsuccessfully to put it back in my pocket. I gaped at the man and monitored the boy, waiting for sudden movements.

"NO. MORE." The man pointed at my wallet.

What a lovely bloke. I took out another small note and held both out to him.

"MORE. More money. You are rich." His eyes darted towards my wallet, and the boy crept around me. In an instant, the man stepped towards me and his hand went down to his belt. Metal gleamed.

The next thing I knew, I'd lost sight of the boy and my wallet had been snatched.

I spun round to see Sally, my wallet in her hand, speedily walking towards two soldiers. Before I could process what was happening, the man grabbed my right arm with one hand, and his other hand pulled the metallic object out of his belt. *This is how I die.* I closed my eyes and waited for the inevitable.

No! I suddenly thought, my survival instincts kicking in. *I won't go down without a fight.*

In a rush of adrenaline, I raised my fist and punched out only to hit thin air. I slowly lifted my eyelids. The man now stood a few feet away from me. The boy said something to him then lunged forward and snatched the two small notes from my hand. And then they both fled back into the souks.

Fear kept me rooted to the spot, and it took me a minute to slow down my breathing. I bent over.

"Sally to the rescue. Again."

I scrutinised her from my prone position. "Eh?" Sally ambled back, while the soldiers turned back around.

"Well, they would've had your wallet but for me."

"Babe, you took my wallet and left me. That wasn't rescuing me. You left me to die."

She shook her head. "Why do I bother?"

"Sorry, I'm feeling overwhelmed by what just happened. They could have killed us." I slowly rose. A thumping in my head accompanied the shakiness of my legs.

"But they didn't."

No, but it had triggered something. A memory. I'd been lost in Marrakesh before, with Dawn, seven years earlier. That time, we'd found our way out, into a square with taxis. She wouldn't have sex for the rest of the holiday, as a punishment for me, for getting us lost. A typical reaction from her. I'd jumped into the nearest one and pulled Dawn in with me. I couldn't believe I'd made the same mistake again. But they say history repeats itself.

And that idiots are destined to repeat their mistakes.

I'd been making a point of not thinking about Dawn, the woman I'd been head over heels in love with. The woman who'd destroyed my trust and broken my heart. After our break-up, I had a nervous breakdown. Yet here I was again, her on my mind and remembering why I'd relegated her to the dark recesses of my brain.

Clearly, I had some recovery work to do.

~

A month later, I woke to Sally shaking me roughly. "Huh, what's happening?" I smacked my lips and blinked slowly.

She leant over me and clasped my cheek. "You were shouting for help. Nightmares again?" She furrowed her brow.

The dream was slipping away, but I had one image: I wanted to shout for help, but in my dream, no words came out. "Yeah, bad dream, that's all."

She flicked the switch on her bedside lamp, and I blinked to adjust to the light. "What about?" She stacked her pillows and sat up against them.

I scratched my head and tried to make sense of it. "Not sure. I think I was dreaming about Marrakesh and being trapped. I . . . I'm fine. I'm okay." I sat myself up against the headboard. Something told me the dream went deeper than the Marrakesh issue.

"What, you're still having nightmares about that?"

"When we got lost in the souks—"

"You mean when you got lost in the souks and I got us out."

"Whatever. I assumed the worst of that guy. My gut reaction was to not trust him."

"Well, he was a foreigner, and you can only rely on your own kind."

"Don't start that again." I shook my head and stared at Sally. "I can't stand that stuff. Anyway, am I evil for mistrusting him?"

"Listen to yourself." She looked incredulous. "If anything, I'd say you're too trusting."

I twisted my body towards her. "Why do you say that?"

"Well, what about that ex of yours, what's-her-face."

"What? Dawn?" As painful memories crowded into my head, I quickly shuffled them into a neat little mind box with *Do Not Disturb* written on it.

"Yeah, her." She gazed at me, raised her eyebrows, and gently shook her head. "You were too unquestioning of her and see what she did to you."

"But that was a one-off."

She studied my face. "Was it? Anyway, I told you to give that guy two quid, and you had to reach into your wallet again to fetch more money."

"They'd got us out of the souks, which neither I nor YOU would have been able to do. Tipping was fair."

"Oh, you and fair. This is a big, bad world with bad people, and you need to toughen up."

She had a point there. "That trip to Morocco did get me thinking about me, you, us, and my place in the world."

She raised her eyebrows. "Don't be turning all philosophical on me now."

"I'm not. I think I need professional help. I think I'm suffering from post-traumatic stress disorder or something." I stared at the curtains behind Sally. It wasn't just the Marrakesh incident but also Dawn and my divorce and its aftermath. Rather than deal with any of it, I'd buried the pain and tried to move on. Each new crisis that came along would get added to the pile. It all felt too overwhelming to tackle. I was powerless. "I've not been right since."

I'd considered visiting my doctor, but at my lowest point, after my divorce, he'd prescribed me antidepressants, and all they'd done—besides afflicting me with the unholy trinity of weight gain, loss of libido, and fatigue—was make me fart a hell of a lot more. I didn't stay on them for long, and I vowed to keep my mental health problems away from my doctor in the future. I was in two minds about a therapist; wanting help but fearful of Sally's reaction making matters worse.

"An overreaction. Whatever happened to getting on with life?" She dropped her head back in exasperation. "I don't think visiting a shrink is a brilliant idea. They'll make everything worse. When has talking about feelings and emotions helped anyone?" She looked at me. "It was just a nightmare. We all experience them."

"I don't know. Maybe you're right." I collapsed onto my pillows. Right to be wary of her response.

Except I wasn't so sure. Drinking to drown out the nightmares had become standard. And during the day, I often found myself biting down on my lip and clenching my fists to quell bursts of pure rage.

"Of course, I'm right. So where are we going next?"

I suddenly felt as if someone were pressing all their weight into my sternum.

"You've just heard," Sally said with a scoff, standing from her chair at the dining table. "America is loosening up on the restrictions. Before long, the place will be just like every other country, with a McDonald's on every corner, high streets dominated by chains, and we'll have missed the chance to visit the real Cuba. Plus, you're a commie. Thought you'd be right at home."

I stood too. "I'm not a communist. At least I don't think I am." I had no clue anymore. I used to know my politics, but over the last few years, my faith in my principles had taken a beating. Nowadays I questioned whether I was a socialist or a capitalist or, worse, a liberal democrat.

I slumped back into my chair. Sally sat down next to me and took my hand. "The choice is yours. Cuba or you and I are done. And this time forever."

I twisted towards her. A real-life ultimatum. "I . . . I . . . Is this your way of finding yourself, like a midlife crisis?"

"Of course not. I know who I am and what I am." She sneered.

Did she, though? Her actions said otherwise. I had to push. "What's happening with us? We're trapped in this pattern of breaking up, you wanting space, me chasing after you, you pushing me away, and then us finally getting back together because you realise you want or need me."

She snorted. "Don't flatter yourself."

I leaned in closer. "I'm not. It's who we've become. But is this the solution? Travelling to Cuba? I had a breakdown after Marrakesh. I'm not sure I can do this."

Though I did want to travel again, Marrakesh still weighed heavily on my psyche.

She shook her head. "You always have to be so overdramatic. You got scared. Nothing more or less."

"What about me? What's in this Cuba trip for me?"

"*You*"—she thrust her finger into my chest—"get *me*. You'll be with me having an adventure. One you'll never forget, with or without therapy." She laughed. "In the Caribbean, too."

Why couldn't she be content to visit a tourist resort in the Canaries or somewhere like that? Somewhere safe. Not somewhere halfway around the world.

As if reading my mind, she continued. "Plus, it's one of the safest places you could ever visit. Extraordinarily little crime. That's one benefit of being in a dictatorship. People are scared to mug you."

"But won't they lock us up for being spies?"

She scoffed again. "Tourism is one of its biggest sectors. They rely on it. They need people like us."

I wanted to say no. "Can I think about it?"

She held my gaze. "Two weeks, otherwise I'll make alternative travel companion arrangements. This is what I want. I need this. It'll shake us up. Escape out of your comfort zone," she said, looking at me steadily. "Travel will be the making of you."

Or quite possibly the breaking.

5

THE INQUISITION

A week after Sally issued her ultimatum, I found myself headed to a meditation group in South West London. Sean and Paddy had invited me. I'd met them through a mutual friend at a summer garden party, and now they were two of my best mates. Both were colourful characters with a history of crime and alcohol and drug abuse. They'd turned their lives around many years ago and now extolled the virtues of meditation. My brain had been in overdrive for days, and I hoped the experience would help me quieten my mind long enough for me to make my decision about Cuba.

I hadn't told Sally about the group as I knew she wouldn't approve. According to her, hippy nonsense like meditation made people mentally ill and there was nothing that hard work and pulling yourself up by your bootstraps wouldn't resolve.

I'd read somewhere that humans have about six thousand thoughts per day. I reckon at that point in my life I was closer to having sixty thousand. My brain's constant whirring exhausted me, and the issue wasn't helped by my living and working in a city that never slowed down.

At the venue, a huge old building owned by Buddhists, I walked in the main entrance and down a hallway to find myself outside a large community hall. As I entered, a bald, skinny bloke with a skeletal face confronted me. "Please put your shoes over here." He pointed towards a cupboard.

"Why?"

He clasped his hands and bowed slightly. "You are setting foot in a sacred place."

I stared into the dark abyss that doubled as a shoe store. Then I looked back at him and wrinkled my nose.

"They'll be safe." He smiled.

I was more worried about my smelly socks than my shoes being taken. One had a hole in the bottom, so no one in their right mind would want them. But, not wanting to make a fuss, I complied. In doing so, I got a whiff that hit the back of my throat and made me cough. I studied the bloke's face for a reaction, but he was inscrutable.

Scanning the hall, I saw I had two options: a chair or a cushion on the floor. Everybody, including Sean and Paddy, sat cross-legged on the cushions, but who or what had been on them concerned me. Plus, the cross-legged position appeared a bit too New Age for me. After my nan died, I'd joined the ranks of lapsed Catholics, seeing no reason to practice anymore. I had no desire to worship a God who'd let her suffer so much. But through my friendships, I'd become a little more open to personal growth and spirituality.

I spotted two middle-aged women with dreadlocks. Lots of blokes with long grey hair and beards. I stroked my hairless chin and had a mini freak-out at the thought of being sat still for thirty minutes with a bunch of strangers. What if I emptied my mind and realised, *I'm nuts*? What if all I could meditate on was Marrakesh, Sally's ultimatum, or, worse still, Dawn? I sometimes had bouts of social anxiety. What if I farted aloud and people stared at me? This would be the longest half hour of my life. But Paddy and Sean swore by it, saying the practice had transformed them. I hoped this could be true for me too.

I grabbed one of the chairs at the back and sat down. Seconds later, a woman about my age sat next to me.

Overcome by a rush of bravery, I spoke to her. "My first time." I stretched my back. No response. "Heard lots of positive experiences about this." I winked at her, aiming to come across as nonchalant. I probably came across as a little odd. Still nothing. "What about you? Come here often?" I winced.

She stared ahead. "My first meditation experience fucked me up." My whole body tensed. "I was in a Buddhist monastery for a week of silence in Thailand and lost my mind."

I twisted towards her. "That was your first experience?"

She eyeballed me. "Yeah." I averted my gaze first. Of course, I had to sit next to the over-sharer.

A bell rang out, and a hush followed.

The guy leading the meditation was good-looking and softly spoken. All in attendance clung to his every word. Except me. I listened sceptically. Speaking about the benefits of meditation, he claimed that as well as reducing stress, aiding sleep, and reducing anxiety, it helped people get over addictions and generated more kindness in the world. And this was all backed by science. I wasn't sold on those last two points, and on whether science was involved. He prowled the front of the hall on a raised platform then took his seat on an elaborately embroidered cushion. "Close your eyes."

As I did so, I tried to suppress a cough in the completely silent room but choked on my efforts. I caught a whiff of my feet again and hoped others wouldn't.

"Concentrate on your breathing."

I breathed. I noticed I breathed. And then I wondered what would happen if I stopped concentrating on my breath. Would it stop and never start again?

"Your thoughts are not you. They just pass through your mind, like clouds in the sky on a sunny day."

Whose thoughts are they, if not mine?

"Let them come without judgement. If you feel anything, just acknowledge them and let them go. They don't define you."

Will I hit that deadline on my report? Is that woman beside me attractive? Wonder what Dawn is doing nowadays? Does she miss me? Piss off, Dawn. Who invited you here? What a fantastic place to steal shoes and umbrellas.

Was I meditating? I peeked through one eye. As far as I could tell, everybody else's eyes were shut. I closed them again.

"Imagine you're sat on the top of the highest mountain in the world."

What the actual hell. I was scared of heights. *Will there be enough oxygen? Will frostbite eat away my toes before they drop off?*

"Look at how blue the sky is, on top of the highest mountain in the world."

Thick grey clouds hide mine. Snow is falling heavily. How the hell am I going to escape from this mountain?

It went on like this for approximately thirty minutes. One of the most unsettling and uncomfortable experiences of my life. Another bell rang, signalling the end of our meditation. I exhaled with relief, feeling no benefits. At least now I could go for a meal with Sean and Paddy.

"Talk to your neighbours about your experience." The hum of quiet conversation rose in the space.

Seriously? The lady next door who freaked out in Thailand. No, thank you. Mental note: avoid Thailand at all costs.

I made my excuses and waited near the shoes for Sean and Paddy.

Minutes later, Sean approached, his arms open. His frame was imposing—he spent lots of time in the gym. I often felt inferior next to him, with my flabby middle-aged spread. "There he is, ya big dick," he said.

I held out my arms as well and squinted. "Whoa there. The lights must have bounced off your bald spot and blinded me."

"Har-har, you funny man." He grabbed me tight and hugged me.

As Sean released me, Paddy stepped forward. "Come here." He pulled me into his bear-like grip and squeezed the life out of me. "You okay?"

I nodded, cleared my throat, and caught my breath.

"Who the hell cut your hair," Paddy said, pointing at my head and grinning.

I stroked my head. "Why? Sally says I suit it."

"Ooooh, Sally says—" Sean cut himself off and turned to Paddy. "Hang on a minute." He frowned and looked at me. "I thought she dumped you?"

"Don't tell us you're back with her?" Paddy punched my arm.

"Ow."

"Just a tap, mate."

I'd hate to be on the receiving end of his real punch. "Yeah, we may get back together." I peered downwards and shuffled. "She's given me an ultimatum—spend Christmas with her in Cuba or we're over forever this time."

"I hope you told her to do one," Sean said, pointing an accusatory finger.

I shook my head. "I'm not sure what to do. I love her, and relationships require hard work. Yes?" I looked at my friends for confirmation. They only furrowed their brows. "But after Marrakesh, I don't fancy going somewhere foreign, especially over the holidays."

"Yeah," Paddy said, "love needs time and effort—from both sides. But come on. You two split up and get back together every couple of months."

Sean leant forward. "Let me guess. She dumped you. You chased after her. She pulled away. You begged her to get back together. Right?"

Damn, a bit on the nose. I looked down again and felt prickles of anxiety rise up my legs and arms. "Not exactly."

"What part was wrong?"

"Well, erm, I didn't beg her. She contacted me." I scratched my head.

"To give you an ultimatum. So, the rest was true. I knew it."

I sighed and shrugged dramatically. "But I love her, and I can't afford for this one to fail. Not after all my other failed relationships."

"That's a lot of pressure you're putting on yourself, Kevin," Paddy said, grabbing my arm gently. "All this love for her and none for you. I hate to say this, but you look like crap. Stressed. Are you taking care of yourself?" He paused. "What the hell is that stench?"

"Is that the man you want to be?" Sean said. He put a hand on my shoulder. "Always chasing her?" He frowned.

"Yeah, you're right, Paddy, what is that stink?"

My face flushing, I spied my socks and clenched my fists. "No and no. But how else can I do this? I need her. Okay, I'm conscious I'm looking ragged, but—"

"Mate." Paddy gripped my arm more tightly. "You need you."

"Oh, you two don't understand," I said, meeting their stares. "Can't you comprehend how important this is to me? Without her, I'm nothing, but the idea of going to Cuba petrifies me. No wonder I'm a little bedraggled. And I can do without the piss-taking and telling me how shit I look. I'm at the end of my tether!" I huffed in frustration and turned away. They had no idea what I was going through. They'd been with the same women for ages.

Paddy gripped my arm again and stepped into my vision, piercing me with his gaze. He rubbed his dark stubble, which was flecked with grey. "We're concerned about you, mate. We've not seen or heard from you for ages."

"Well, I've had a lot on my plate with all this going on." This had been a mistake, coming here. "Sally's right about you both. You're not my real friends." I brushed Paddy away.

"Bros before—"

I interrupted Sean before he could finish his sentence. "Please don't call Sally what I think you were going to say. This is not helping me at all."

"Neither is your smelly socks, mate." He wafted his hand under his nose, which he wrinkled in disgust.

I shifted my weight forward, trying to move my feet deeper into the carpet.

"Who's paying for this holiday?" Sean asked.

"Reckon you'll be splashing the cash," Paddy said. "You told me before that you pay for everything."

"I haven't even said I'm going yet, but if we do, I imagine I'll pay. And organise everything." I waved dismissively. "But to be honest, I'm out of pocket and out of my depth. The more I think about it, the more I reckon this is a terrible idea." I rubbed my face as my mind turned to my credit card bills and bank balance. Financial worries—another problem to add to the pile.

"Well, don't go," Paddy said.

"Who are you doing this for?" Sean asked.

"Me. Both of us." I sighed. "Okay, for her. I can't lose her. I'll do whatever is necessary to hold on to her."

"To the detriment of yourself?" Paddy asked.

The questions, the teasing, the insinuations—it was all too much. Maybe they understood better than I wanted to let on. "NO! Don't you see that being with Sally benefits me!" I yelled, balling my hands into fists. Meanwhile, people floated past, most of them beaming and glowing. Where had I gone wrong?

"Lot going on for you, Mr Kelly," Sean said. "How is all this for you?"

"If I make this relationship work, I'll be happy," I said defiantly.

"How's that worked out for you so far?"

"YOU DON'T UNDERSTAND ME OR US."

With that, I turned around and stormed down the hallway to the front door. Then I glanced down at my socks.

Crap.

I trudged back in and picked up my shoes. Peering up, I saw Paddy and Sean shaking their heads at me. My heart sank. I couldn't communicate what was going on with me, and I hated that we were arguing.

I left feeling more alone than ever.

The inquisition didn't stop there. A couple of days later, I met Yolanda, my work wife, for lunch. Our team had designated her as such due to the way we bickered and fought but backed each other to the hilt. Sally knew about Yolanda but didn't "see her as a threat." Her words, not mine. My and Yolanda's relationship was based on banter, insults, and an underlying mutual affection. And right now, I desperately needed her advice.

As I approached our usual spot, the Turkish restaurant not far from our workplace in Lewisham, I spotted her waiting outside. She was easy to spot, given that she was wearing her monstrosity of a bobble hat—it was mustard yellow, and the huge bobble sprouted wool in various directions.

Yolanda pointed at her watch. "Where have you been? You're late." Meeting on our lunch break meant that time was precious.

"Hi, how are you," I said sarcastically, then pointed to her head and made an exaggerated look of disgust. "Why are you wearing *that*?"

"Urgh, okay. Hi, how are you? *Why are you late?*" She made a tremendous show of poking her watch.

"Sorry, was messaging Sally."

"What did that bitch want? I thought you two were finished?"

"Please don't call her names. It's complicated."

"Always is with you. Would be simple with me, darling." She grinned.

"I don't want to talk about that."

Yolanda ran her hands down her heavy winter coat and stared at me with her menacing brown eyes. "*Well.* You're not going to tell me how beautiful I am?"

She'd always feigned attraction to me. At least I hoped she was pretending, as I'd never felt that way towards her. Maybe we were proof that men and women could be friends without the messiness of sexual chemistry. I looked her up and down. "Meh, acceptable. And for the love of God, take that bobble hat off, please."

She scoffed and took off the offending item, revealing her close-cropped hair, dyed gold.

She linked her arm in mine, but I wriggled free—no simple task, as she had an Amazonian stature—and flung her hand to one side to grab the door. "Shall we?" I ushered her in.

A gentleman in a lumberjack-esque shirt greeted us. Bloody hipsters were nicking all the hospitality jobs nowadays. The last time I'd taken a hipster waiter's advice, I'd ended up taking Sally to Margate, resulting in a deep distrust of them.

We were seated at a table for two. I scanned the busy establishment and noticed some other people from work three tables away. "Hi, we're not a couple," I shouted over to them.

"Stop denying it. We adore each other. We're totally in

love." As Yolanda said this, she went to stroke my face, but being heavy-handed, she ended up slapping me.

I flung my face to the side. "Please, not today, darling. Don't hit me again."

Our colleagues smiled weakly and then resumed their conversation.

The lumberjack/waiter appeared with a jug of water and filled our tumblers. "Are you ready to order?"

"No, but could you bring some garlic bread while we peruse the menu?" I picked up the menus from the middle of the table and handed one to Yolanda. As the waiter departed, I turned to my friend. "So, you been to any good funerals lately?"

"Yeah, an auntie's funeral last week."

I took a sip of water. "What, a real aunty or a pretend one?"

Her laugh reminded me of a high-pitched machine gun, and it filled the room. Just being in her presence made me feel lighter and less stressed out. Why did I feel like this with Yolanda but on edge with Sally so much of the time? I fancied Sally, but surely that couldn't be the full explanation. Me and Yolanda get on great, love to joke around and no subject is taboo in our banter.

"Now no more. What's going on with you and that woman?"

The waiter arrived and placed a plate of garlic bread on the table. I thanked him and asked for a few more minutes. He nodded and left us to it.

"Now you stop. She has a name." I scratched my head. The ability to marshal my thoughts into coherent speech was becoming increasingly elusive. Where to start? "I'm confused," I managed to blurt. "We split up and now she's given me an ultimatum: go to Cuba for Christmas or we're done. Finished. Over."

"What are you going to do?"

I tore off a piece of garlic bread. "Feels like an impossible choice. I want her, but I want to spend Christmas here in the safety of the UK." I shoved the bread in my mouth and chewed.

"Are you even happy with her?"

"Oh, don't you start." I met Yolanda's gaze. "Everybody seems to think she's bad for me, but she's the best thing to ever happen to me. Without her . . . well, it doesn't bear thinking about."

"Kevin, have you seen yourself in the mirror?" she said bluntly, putting a hand on my arm. "You're unshaven, your clothes are all rumpled, you're a mess."

"I just hate decisions like this. I'll be fine once I decide. First-rate again." Even as I said the words, a voice in my head scoffed.

I scanned the menu and nodded to Yolanda to do the same. When the waiter returned, I ordered garlic mushrooms to start and lamb kebab. Yolanda ordered olives, garlic mushrooms, and doner kebab. And we each ordered a beer.

After placing the menus back in their holder, Yolanda studied me for a few moments. "Not sure I even fancy you anymore." She chuckled then sucked on her fingers one by one while making eye contact with me. I glanced away and blushed.

"Yeah, right," I said, shaking my head and laughing. "You know you do."

She became serious again. "You're right, I do, but I'm worried about you. We all are."

"Who's we?" I sat bolt upright. I hated being talked about.

Yolanda squirmed in her seat. "People at work. Your friends."

I threw myself back in my chair. "Oh, great, now people at the office are talking about me." *Brilliant.* "That's all I need."

The waiter arrived with our olives and beer. I immediately

drank half of mine and indicated he should bring another. I clocked Yolanda gawping at me and avoided her gaze. "Can we talk about something else? Your latest funeral or something." She'd worried me with her throwaway comment about people at work. Would she talk to them about this?

"Well, I have another one next week. An aunty."

"Another funeral? Real or fake aunty?"

"They're all real." Yolanda slapped my arm, and I nearly fell out of my chair.

"Take it easy, tiger," I said. Yolanda offered me an olive. I screwed up my face and pretended to vomit. "Yuk."

"What?" She popped it into her mouth.

"I hate them. Horrible things."

"Olives? Why?"

"Oh, long story."

She pulled the stone out of her mouth, put it in the olives bowl, and ate another one. I gagged a little. "We've got time," she said.

"Okay. The first time I went abroad, to Greece, I was on a flight that served meals." A family holiday with my parents and annoying sister. Well, she was then. Nowadays, we were close. That first trip abroad had felt like a real adventure except without the stress and hassle. I went to Greece a couple more times after that, along with Spain and America. I loved travelling but favoured the more popular tourist destinations when doing so. I took a swig of beer, and then another. "It was a salad. Not what I wanted. But then I saw it had Maltesers on top." I poured the fresh beer that the waiter had just brought into my glass and sipped it. "Popped one in my mouth. Turns out it wasn't lovely chocolate but one of those monstrosities." I gestured to the olive bowl and grimaced.

"Why the hell did you think they'd serve Maltesers on a salad?"

"Because I was fifteen, never been abroad before, and

stupid." I tapped the side of my head. "Ever since, I've not been able to stand them."

Yolanda gawped at me, shook her head, and burst into laughter. "You idiot."

"Yeah, right, tell me about it."

The waiter arrived with our main courses. I ordered another beer. "And another for you?" I asked, looking at Yolanda. She shook her head. Pity. I was hoping she'd drink more so I'd feel less self-conscious about how much I was drinking.

As we ate, we bantered for several minutes. Then Yolanda turned serious again. She lowered her eyebrows. "So, what decision will you make?"

I shrugged. "The only reason I want to go to Cuba is to keep Sally happy and to stop her from dumping me."

Yolanda sipped her beer. "I hear the weather's fantastic—and don't forget mojitos." She held up her glass.

"But there are lots of things that scare me."

"Like?"

"Like what if the holiday is a disaster and she dumps me anyway, the plane crashes, rabid dogs, getting mugged, my lodger having wild parties while I'm away . . ."

Yolanda's brow creased.

I swigged back more beer. "I know, none of this is rational." I leant backwards then shot forward again, pointing my finger and nodding vigorously. "Mosquitoes, there's bound to be loads of bitey insects. Plus, crap internet. And I always get sunburnt."

"All part of the joy and adventure of travelling abroad."

"Is it? What about diarrhoea, not speaking Spanish, or getting lost?"

"Easy just look up how to say 'Hello, I'm lost, and I've shat my pants'."

I slammed my glass down on the table. "Brilliant. Why didn't I talk to you before?"

Yolanda had been no help, and decision day was fast approaching, with only a few days left. I had to face it. I'd made my decision the moment the ultimatum had been issued.

6
ROGER

Thud. My head smacked against the passenger window. "Ow."
Smack. "Ouch."
Thump. "OW. OUCH."
"Are you all right, darling?" Sally asked from the back seat.
I half-turned and waved at her. "I'm fine, banged my head on the glass. I'll be fine. Everything is fine."
After I decided to go to Cuba, another decision was made: to accept a lift to the airport from Sally's friend Roger. As we careered the wrong way around a roundabout, fellow drivers flashing their headlamps and beeping their horns at us all the while, I knew it'd been the wrong decision. Roger's nickname, "the alky" (alcoholic), should have been a clue.
Oblivious to my predicament and oncoming traffic, Roger carried on, and I wondered if I'd even make it to Cuba. Maybe for the best? Better to die here than abroad at the hands of some unknown assailant. At least I knew Roger.
Sally was engrossed in her phone, blissfully unaware of the danger to her life posed by Roger's erratic driving. I left her to it—sometimes best not to know. Plus, this was all my fault anyway, if Sally was to be believed. My car, which was parked

outside Sally's house, had failed to start on account of a dead battery. I'd left all the lights on.

She'd raged about my stupidity and idiocy, and Roger had been on hand to give us a lift. He seemed to relish the opportunity to rescue Sally, who then told me Andy would fix the car while we were away. The mere mention of his name made jealousy well up in me. I hadn't accepted the lift from the alky, though. That fault lay with Sally.

Roger was a former colleague who, according to him, was stuck in a loveless marriage. He often took refuge at Sally's, where he drowned his sorrows and hid from his wife. He was also possibly in love with Sally.

In his early sixties, Roger had a mop of white hair that sprouted chaotically from his scalp. He was about six feet, both high and wide, and he wore short-sleeved shirts all year round. His body burst out of every nook and cranny of his too-small shirt. He also had a habit of not buttoning up the top three buttons. His white chest hair flowed through the gaps. He said he didn't feel the cold. I assumed the enormous amount of alcohol he consumed inoculated him.

He was affable, not a mean bone in his body. It's just, well, he wasn't the best person to accept a lift from.

The roundabout incident was the worst infringement of the Highway Code on the journey, but not the only one. There were a couple of failed stops at red lights and a failure to check both ways at a junction, too. Thankfully, after two circuits the wrong way round, we made our way to the correct side of the road.

I later worked out that Roger had taken a wrong turn onto the M25, London orbital motorway. We were supposed to be heading towards Gatwick Airport but at some point, found ourselves on the way to Heathrow, in the complete opposite direction. Despite this, I had to admit that Roger was a far better driver than I. But then, most people are. I passed my driving test on the sixth attempt.

Once we were on the right track, the journey took an even more dangerous turn: Roger began regaling us with stories of his latest conquests on the 'meet a granny' website he was subscribed to. He "wasn't getting any from his wife", he explained, and he had "an extraordinarily high sex drive". Way too much information for my liking. He referred to his wife as "the Old Dog." Who knows, maybe she was on a "grab a grandad" site and had nicknamed him "the Old Bastard."

Forgive me for not including a link to the site but take my word for it—it exists. Roger insisted on showing me a picture of his latest conquest, Doreen from Bexleyheath. In my younger days, the Grafton in Liverpool provided that service. On 'grab a granny' night, fresh-faced young men would mingle with older women hoping for a late-night liaison. I never made an appearance at the legendary place, but some of my mates did and their stories shocked and awed me.

As Roger's stories flowed, the copious numbers of empty wine bottles on the floor clinked and knocked against each other. *Probably explains why we went the wrong way around a roundabout twice and ended up headed to Heathrow*, I thought.

We arrived at our destination an hour later than planned. Thankfully, Sally and I were staying in a hotel airport that night, as our flight was early in the morning. I'd thought this would make the overall journey less stressful. We all make mistakes. At least we'd arrived in one piece.

I watched as Roger drove away and wondered whether he'd make it home okay, especially as he'd forgotten to put his headlights on. I jumped up and down and pointed to them, but he must have thought I was waving goodbye, as he just waved back then sped off into the night.

Was I doing the right thing? The argument with Sally over my car and Roger's alcohol-fuelled driving were giving me second thoughts about the whole trip, and it hadn't even officially started.

That evening, I stared out of the window in our room, gazing at the spectacular view of the runways and trying to calm my nerves. A plane took off, red lights on its undercarriage blinking against the starry black night. Would I die on this trip? Worse, would I fail in my quest to woo Sally?

When I turned around, I found Sally already in bed, under the duvet—a titillating sign. Excitement overtook my anxiety. But then she picked up the remote control and switched the telly on. Not quite what I'd hoped for.

"Come to bed and watch this with me."

"What is this?" I said, glancing at the telly as I made my way to the bed.

She looked incredulous. "You mean you've never seen it before?"

"That's why I'm asking you. I always ask you when I've seen it before."

She waggled a finger at me. "Now, now, darling, no need to be sarcastic. It's Luther."

I scratched my head. "Luther? Never seen it. Any good?"

"Yes, brilliant," she said, clapping. "I love it and you will too. Come on." She patted the spot next to her. I hopped onto the bed feeling my hope deflating. So much for a snog. Or more.

"Phwoar. Hm, corrr."

I looked at Sally and frowned. Unusual, these guttural and carnal noises coming from her. I couldn't work out whether my luck was in or she was choking on something.

"Isn't he gorgeous? Look at him. He's so handsome."

I stared at the screen and located the source of her grunts. "What, him? The detective guy? We've had this conversation before, darling. I don't find men attractive."

She half-turned to me. "But you can still have a view on whether you think he's handsome."

"What's his name?"

She raised her eyebrows. "You mean to say you don't recognise him?"

"Of course. That's why I'm asking you."

"Idris Elba. How can you not know who he is, darling? Everybody does!"

I wondered if I might need to book Sally an appointment at Specsavers. Having said that, I had a vague recollection of women at work talking about him in similar rushed, breathless tones.

I patted her legs under the duvet and rose to do a triple-check of all our documents and arrangements. All was in order, thank God. My time as a civil servant had been of use after all. I gave Sally her copies of everything, but my doing so didn't attract the carnal noises she'd emitted earlier. Her eyes stayed focused on the telly. How rude. Who wouldn't be aroused by a run-through of an itinerary and its accompanying documents? Sometimes I didn't understand her.

I didn't understand women, full stop.

But I reminded myself that this holiday would be my key to happily ever after. I'd done my best to bury my phobias, insecurities, and worries in the dark recesses of my mind. A final break-up would surely trigger even more stuff that I'd buried even deeper. I was all in for this trip.

I nipped into the toilet to pop a blue pill, Viagra, hoping that Sally would be frisky after her show was finished. I'd been taking the pills since the beginning of our relationship because of problems I'd experienced previously with the old fellow—not standing to attention when I wanted him to, for example, and then standing to attention at the most inappropriate times.

I was fingering the tablet when I heard Sally's phone ring.

"Hi, Rog, babe. Can't talk long. He's in the bathroom. Aw, thanks for the lift. So sweet of you, angel. Yes . . ."

I popped it in my mouth and stepped towards the door.

"You're right. Wish I could have got out of it. But I've spent all that money and . . ."

I frowned and put my head closer to the door.

"I'll be fine."

Pressed my ear against the gap between the door and the frame.

"Yeah, single beds, thank God. I insisted."

Cracked the door ajar, my frown deepening.

"He knows better than to try any of that nonsense. Must go, I think I can hear him coming. Love you. Bye."

I swung open the door and strode into the bedroom area. "Hey, babe. Everything okay?" Everything was far from okay. Why on earth had Sally lied to Roger?

Sally smiled. "Roger checking on me. You know what he's like. Treats me like I'm his daughter."

I walked towards my side of the double bed. "That was good of him."

Daughter? Really? What the hell had I just overheard?

7
WHERE'S FIDEL?

Having barely got any sleep after the cockroach incident, I stumbled behind Sally to a restaurant in our hotel that served a breakfast buffet. It looked nice enough. The tables were covered in white tablecloths, and a large arched window overlooked a garden. The floor was a chequerboard of white and black. At the entrance, two staff stood chatting.

"Excuse me," I asked. "Is this breakfast?"

"Breakfast there," said one of the sullen-looking young women, pointing inside the restaurant. Both wore tight white blouses and khaki miniskirts.

"Where can we sit?"

She scowled. "Sit. Yes." Then she went back to gossiping with her equally petulant colleague.

"Where can we sit?"

The woman tutted and stared at me with utter disdain. "Yes. Sit." She nodded in the general direction of the dining area.

Sally touched my shoulder. "What's happening, darling?"

"Not sure. I think we just occupy any table."

"Can we take a place?" Sally said. "I'm hungry and need my coffee."

They would not defeat me. "Hi, sorry to interrupt. But can we sit anywhere? Any table?" This time, the other woman turned to roll her eyes, tut, and stare at me with derision. She said something in Spanish to her compatriot and then forced a smile at me. "Sit. Yes." She shooed me away, reminding me of my cockroach jig. I suddenly felt bad for the cockroach.

"Come on, Sal, let's grab some seats." We found a table in front of the window and sat down.

"No. NO. Sir. Madam. Please, I show you." This waitress was older and friendlier, with permed brown hair and too much make-up.

"Not here? No?" I tapped the table with a finger.

"No," she said, with urgency in her tone. "This table is for four. You are two. You must not sit here. Please. Follow me." She motioned us with her hand.

I studied my surroundings. The place was empty. "Can we stay here?"

"No. No. Please come." She clasped her hands, and her eyes darted from left to right, looking for that someone who'd created the two-people-on-two-person-tables rule. A person to be respected and scared of. I saw her eyes meet those of an officious-looking man with a waxed moustache. He gestured to an empty two-person table. When we sat down, he nodded at her and turned his attentions, likely to other infractions.

I looked up at the waitress as she turned to leave. "Two coffees, please?"

"No. Erm." She gestured to a waiter on the other side of the room, who was holding a coffee pot. Then I noticed tears slowly rolling down her cheeks, leaving streaks of black mascara in their wake.

"Are you okay?" I asked, concerned that she was about to be reprimanded by the moustache.

"*Sí*, yes, okay." She wiped her cheeks with her hand and

then produced some tissue from her skirt. "This morning, I fight with my husband and I say to him, no more. I give you all the love and nothing back. Now is time for me." She wiped a couple more tears away. "Always him and the children get all the love and me, never any back. Now I care for me. Love me. Any left, maybe some after that." She straightened her skirt and smoothed down her blouse, giving a little cough.

I was taken aback. And a little impressed. "Wow, I hope it works."

"Work? Why yes, this is how will be. So yes, will work."

"Well, good luck."

She turned and walked away.

Sally slowly shook her head at me. "You have a knack for getting involved with other women, don't you?"

Was she serious? "No. I just asked a question and she provided too much information. Not my fault."

"I should be like that woman, looking after me for a change rather than putting all my energies into you and Harry."

I swallowed. I barely got by on the attention Sally paid me. "I'm sure she'll be back looking after everyone again soon. Seems like she's just having a bad day."

After an angry man eventually served us coffee, Sally brushed the hair on my forehead with her hand. "Aww, I love your hair like this. I hated that buzz cut. You look handsome now."

"Don't you mean more handsome?"

She smiled and ignored my comment. "Is that the new shirt I bought you?"

I gaped down at it. "Don't know?" It was. She'd chosen every top I owned now. All part of her makeover of me.

"You look much healthier with a tan, too. More refined than when you were that bluey-white colour." She continued smiling. "Do you remember that?"

I did. And I didn't want her to know that I preferred my

new hairstyle, that I knew I was wearing the new shirt, and that, yes, I looked better with a tan. Although I wouldn't admit it to her, I loved being told how to improve my appearance. I didn't understand how to do any of that—better she had control. Woman's touch and all that. I also knew this stuff made her happy. Well, not happy. Happier. Well, maybe less unhappy.

Out of nowhere, a dull cacophony filled the restaurant. I looked up to see the space filling with loud elderly guests. They seemed incapable of talking at a normal volume.

Sally looked disapprovingly around the room. "Let's go."

My tummy rumbled. "But we've not eaten yet. I'm starving."

She stood. "Come on, you wanted an adventure, and we've not even set foot outside the hotel yet. We have an entire city to explore."

Did I want an adventure? Or was that just her? "What, just walk out of here and traipse around Havana? I'm not sure that's a great idea."

"Come on, you're the mighty explorer now. Let's go."

A voice inside my head screamed *No!*

Panic stations were on full alert. I hadn't thought this through. I had nothing booked. I rose, but not before grabbing half a loaf of bread, a stick of butter, a pot of jam, and a knife, off an empty table as we left. No sense going hungry while I figured it out.

Back in our room, sat on the bed I munched on my bread and jam as Sally disappeared into the bathroom, where her phone was charging. My eye was caught by an information sheet on the nightstand. She quickly re-emerged. "Still no internet. How about Wi-Fi?"

"According to this, there's a Wi-Fi zone in the hotel lobby,"

I said, grabbing the piece of paper from the nightstand and waving it at her. "I suspect when they say, 'Wi-Fi zone', they mean that if you stand still in a certain spot, you can access enough Wi-Fi to send a message and maybe download a couple too. We can check it out when we go down."

"Let's go then." Sally stood at the door.

My nerves kicked up again. Was a relaxing day too much to ask for? *Dream on.*

Back on the ground floor in the antiquated lift, I waved my phone in the air and found a spot where my phone got a half-decent connection. I ushered Sally over. "Right, don't move and you should be able to send and receive some messages." She turned away from me. "No, you need to stand still." I glanced over Sally's shoulder and noticed she had a full Wi-Fi signal. She turned further, obscuring the screen.

One problem down. Now to solve the one about how to explore Havana safely. I spotted a tourist information desk in a corner of the lobby and made my way over.

"*Hola,*" said one of the women behind the desk.

"Hi . . . Hola." I'd meant to take Spanish lessons but hadn't. The constant making and breaking up with Sally left little time for anything else. My grasp of Spanish was minimal. Read non-existent.

"English, yes?"

"English, yes."

"Would you like to go on a tour of Havana? Starts in thirty minutes, at eleven o'clock."

"Yeah, sounds great. How much?"

"Twenty-five bucks."

I fumbled around in my pocket and handed over the requisite notes.

"Each."

Each? Wow, expensive. But at least we'd be escorted around. That made me feel safe. I handed over the rest.

"Meet your tour guide by the cannon in the gardens at the back of the hotel."

"That way?" I pointed.

"*Sí*, yes, in the back."

I waited for a piece of paper that never came. "Do I need a receipt?"

"No. Goodbye." She dismissed me with her hand.

Well then.

I found Sally rooted to the same spot. Several other tourists were now in the vicinity, all trying to fit into the zone of outside connection. "How are you getting on with your messages?"

"I sent one to my mum. Picked up two messages. Nothing from Harry. Tried to go on Facebook, but my Wi-Fi died. What about you?"

All this way to go on Facebook. I supposed we all had our addictions and time thieves. Mine was the rabbit hole that is YouTube. One minute I'd be watching a video about Everton and an hour later, I'd watched ten videos about My Little Pony without a clue how the hell I got there.

"I booked us on a walking tour of Havana."

"How much did you pay?"

"Twenty-five bucks. Why?"

Her eyes widened. "Darling, that's way too much. Did you try to barter them down?"

I avoided her gaze. "Yes, of course. They asked for fifty bucks." A blatant lie. I'd forgotten about Sally's obsession with negotiating. I hated bartering. I'd much rather pay the money than suffer the shame and embarrassment of haggling and losing. The only time I indulged was when Sally was around. In an attempt to keep her happy.

"Still way too high. In future, leave that to me."

"Okay, darling."

As we had a little time to kill, Sally headed off to the bar in the gardens at the back after handing me her phone to take upstairs and charge. My duty done, I met her in the gardens. We were the only guests around.

"Dos mojitos, por favor," I said to the waiter. At least I knew that much Spanish.

When he returned, I wondered for a nanosecond about the acceptability of drinking a cocktail before eleven in the morning then downed the sugary beverage. Glancing around, I spotted the gigantic cannon. "We need to be over there at eleven," I said, pointing.

"Can't believe how much you paid," Sally said, shaking her head. "We should have wandered around ourselves and spent the money on mojitos."

Madness. Who knew what dangers lay outside the confines of the hotel?

∼

At the cannon, we were joined by two couples, two middle-aged women travelling together, and a bloke on his own. *Poor guy*, I thought. I wondered if his girlfriend had dumped him just before the trip.

The tour guide, a friendly young woman called Juanita, gathered us together. With her dark hair, deep hazel eyes, and short stature, her resemblance to Dawn was frightening. Dawn. There she was in my thoughts again. I shook my head to rid myself of the memories. There was no place in my life or my head for her anymore. Thankfully, Juanita stepped in to interrupt my train of thought. "So, have you got your payment?"

"Oh, I paid the woman at the information desk."

Juanita rolled her eyes and muttered something under her breath in Spanish that sounded like *bastardas*.

"Is everything okay?"

"Yes, yes, it is fine, it is fine," she said, clearly exasperated.

In my experience, whenever a woman said those words,

the situation was far from okay. But I didn't want to press the issue. I'd paid and that was that.

"Follow me."

We headed back through the hotel and out towards the top of the road leading into the main road, where we were met by a dilapidated white minibus.

Sally rolled her eyes. "Seriously, Kevin? Is that our transport today?"

"Looks fine to me. I'm sure it will get us around Havana." Lies. I imagined it falling to pieces as soon as the driver turned the key in the ignition.

"What a heap of crap."

I prayed she wouldn't make a scene.

Leaning against the dirty machine, a middle-aged man with jet-black hair smoking a rolled-up cigarette talked to several taxi drivers. When he saw Juanita, he threw his smoke to the ground and shooed his mates away. They hurried away.

Juanita pointed towards him. "This is Fidel. He will be our driver today."

He smiled and nodded at us. "Hola."

"Hi, Fidel." Noticing I was the only one who'd returned his greeting, I coughed to hide my embarrassment. Sally snorted.

"Please, on the bus," Juanita urged us.

First stop, Revolution Square.

"We will be here for thirty minutes," Juanita said, as the bus ground to a halt 25 minutes after leaving the hotel. "Follow me."

Dutifully we disembarked, and Juanita guided us to a huge open plaza surrounded by greenery. At one end was a multi-lane carriageway sparsely populated with cars. At the opposite end, white government buildings stood in each corner. Evenly spaced lamp posts filled the square. Juanita stopped in front of a tall statue. "First, we have the José Martí Memorial." She gestured towards the statue. "The pre-eminent feature is the star-shaped tower. It's over one hundred metres high and depicts José Martí, a hero in Cuba," she said proudly. "A poet, writer, and revolutionary."

I gazed around the vast plaza. Given that I suffer from acrophobia and agoraphobia—a fear of heights and wide-open spaces, respectively—I tried to calm my jittery nerves by concentrating on Juanita's dulcet tones. Through the trees, a glimpse of panoramic views of the city was almost as breathtaking as my panic.

"Through his writings and political activity, Martí became a symbol of Cuba's bid for freedom from Spain in the nineteenth century," Juanita explained. "He is referred to as the 'Apostle of Cuban Independence'."

Juanita ushered us to the centre of Revolution Square. I took a deep breath and stuck as close to Sally as possible. She didn't seem to notice.

"Construction of the square itself and the José Martí Memorial began during the presidency of Batista and was completed in 1959, which was also the year of the revolution. The revolution has great meaning and significance to the people." Then she pointed out some government offices near the bottom of the plaza. I think she mentioned "interior" and "information". I wished I could concentrate properly. I loved learning stuff like this.

On the sides of two buildings, at the opposite end of the Plaza to the motorway, were pieces of art constructed out of metal. One depicted Che Guevara. The other appeared to be a likeness of Ayatollah Khomeini, the old leader of Iran. *Odd*, I thought. *Why the hell would Cuba feature him in their artwork?* I interrupted Sally, who appeared to be enraptured by Juanita and her knowledge. "Can you see the installations on the sides of the buildings," I whispered, pointing. "One is Che Guevara and the other is Ayatollah Khomeini."

"Aww, you're so intelligent, darling." Sally pecked me on my cheek for being so clever.

I must try to be clever more often, I told myself, wanting to discover what other rewards were on offer for my intelligence.

"On the sides of the Government buildings you will observe memorials of the two most important deceased heroes of the Cuban Revolution," Juanita announced. "Che Guevara, with the quotation *Hasta la Victoria Siempre*, which translates to 'Until the Everlasting Victory, Always', and Camilo Cienfuegos, who is sometimes mistaken for Fidel Castro, with the quotation *Vas Bien, Fidel*, which translates to 'You're doing fine, Fidel'." She giggled. An inside joke amongst Cubans, I assumed.

Sally pulled on my shirt. "I thought you said that was Ayatollah Khomeini?"

Shit. "I misread that one, but I got Che right."

Sally furrowed her brow and walked away.

What the hell? Why did I think that was the old leader of Iran? Why on earth would he be saying, "You're doing fine, Fidel"?

I'd read somewhere that Fidel delivered his legendary four-hour speeches in the square. Standing at his pulpit, he'd lambast and harangue the party faithful. I could only assume he bored them into submitting to his viewpoint. Apparently, up to a million people used to congregate for the speeches. I wondered whether they stood or had chairs. I mean, if they had chairs, that's a lot of chairs. Where would they store them? And four hours with no toilet breaks? I'd never have been able to cope. Yet, there was no record of anyone shouting, "Get on with it!"

I couldn't resist a photo op with Che Guevara's famous face in the background. I did my best raised-fist salute as Sally took a photo. The only problem was that I had a mini panic attack while stood within the vastness of the square, which didn't make for a great photo. My face contorted into a gurn and my knees knocked together. I returned the favour for

Sally, who struck a hand-on-hip duck-face pose. I was glad she seemed to be enjoying herself.

As we piled back on the bus, Sally innocently asked Juanita, "So where does Fidel Castro live now?"

I cringed internally, and there was an excruciatingly awkward silence while Juanita studied Sally carefully, likely weighing her up as a potential assassin. There had been several hundred attempts on Castro's life, although that was according to the man himself, who was hardly unbiased.

Juanita shifted twice in her seat and opened and closed her mouth four times before words came out. "No one knows where the former commander-in-chief lives."

The palpable tension continued to hang in the air. I nudged Sally, hoping she'd take the hint and not ask further questions. She turned to me. I raised my eyebrows exaggeratedly. She turned away. "So, is he still active? Does he still make speeches? What does he do now?"

Clearly, I'd been too subtle.

Juanita paused again, seemingly unwilling to upset one of her tourists but uncomfortable with talking about her exalted leader. She took a deep breath. "The former commander-in-chief is retired, but he holds a special place in Cuban society. He is still active, meets foreign leaders, and occasionally writes."

"Oh, okay, thank you." It appeared Sally was all questioned out. Thank God. Juanita spoke to the driver in Spanish, and the bus rumbled to life.

According to my extensive research, aka Google, my other favourite time thief, the CIA investigated the possibility of planting mollusc shells containing explosives in the ocean where Fidel used to scuba dive and painting them bright colours to attract him. Then, when he got close enough, boom! They also pondered infecting his diving suit with a fungus that would cause a lethal disease or at the very least an irritating skin rash that would force him to apply soothing creams instead of plotting the overthrow of American capitalism.

Another article I'd read said that the CIA tried to encourage one of his ex-girlfriends to kill him. Now this made sense—I know one or two of my exes would love to, at the very least, infect me with an annoying skin fungus. Other attempts to kill Fidel involved poisonous pens, exploding cigars, and bacterial poisons designed to be dissolved in his coffee or tea.

Depending on one's political views, Fidel Castro is either a man of the people and champion of the oppressed or a vile communist/fascist dictator. Or perhaps you've never heard of him. In his youth, he was the spitting image of a young, bearded Liam Neeson. The likeness is uncanny. Who knows, maybe during the Cuban Missile Crisis he phoned JFK to let the US government know he possessed a "particular set of skills." Fidel was also a major player, alleged to have five wives and eleven children.

I wondered if it was bad form to use his name, as Juanita had mouthed "former commander-in-chief," both times. I thought of Voldemort in Harry Potter.

Looking out of the window of the minibus as it travelled the potholed roads, I finally spied some of the famed classic cars, scattered amongst some vehicles that appeared to be barely alive.

Sally pulled at my arm. "Aww, look at those amazing cars. Wish ours had turned up." She stared wistfully at them while I soaked up her crushing disappointment and converted it into a berating of myself for my lack of classic-car-booking skills.

Most of the buildings displayed a mix of colonial and Art Deco architecture, and many of them had scaffolding around them. The extensive building works had been initiated too late for some, which appeared to be way beyond repair. I was particularly struck by the bright blues and pinks interspersed with the greys and beiges. Not quite the caricature of the old Soviet bloc. Here, colours were allowed and encouraged.

Next stop, Plaza de la Catedral.

Stood in the square, I glanced around as Juanita offered details. "The cathedral is called Catedral de San Cristóbal, which, along with the other buildings surrounding the square, dates back to the eighteenth century."

When she was animated, her hands became a whirr of movement—another similarity to Dawn. Trying to ignore the thoughts of my ex only increased my lingering feelings of loss. Tears welled up behind my eyes. I gulped and barely managed to hold them back.

Refocusing on my surroundings, I noticed that the place was bustling with tourists—and locals trying to interact with us. They'd try now and again to approach, but Juanita was adept at spotting them. She'd glare, and they'd walk away to lick their wounds.

Juanita directed us away from the square to a side street and pointed towards a bar so jam-packed with tourists that they spilt out onto the pavement. Several were trying to shove their way in. "This is La Bodeguita del Medio. Ernest Hemingway, the writer, used to come here."

"Did he drink mojitos?" Sally asked.

Juanita pretended not to hear her, though I'm not sure why. Maybe it was a stupid question? Or perhaps it was revenge for Sally's impertinent questions about "you know who"?

I wrapped my arm around Sally. "What's her problem?" I said quietly.

She smiled and adorably wrinkled her nose. "I know, right?"

I pecked her on the cheek. "How are you doing, darling?"

"Good. Loving Havana so far. So much history, and it's different too." She turned her head to look at me. "Thanks for organising this guided tour. Been fascinating so far."

I softened inside. "My absolute pleasure, beautiful."

She squeezed my hand.

By now the Cuban sun was beating down hard, so I slathered on some sun cream, lest I burn. Sally promptly turned her back and stepped away from me, embarrassed by my cack-handed attempts to apply the cream. My chest tightened. Her obvious distancing of herself from me was even more painful after our lovely interaction. Always the push and pull. Connection and separation.

Next, Juanita pointed out the Palacio de los Marquesas de Villalba, built in the 1700s. Once Havana's main post office—an original letterbox remained on the exterior wall—it was now an art gallery where prints and handicrafts were available for purchase. This was the first place I'd seen that sold anything. Perhaps Cuba wasn't the monolithic communist state I'd assumed. Maybe capitalism was making a comeback here. I wanted to explore this aspect of the country more.

We visited an enormous number of squares that day. They loved their squares, the Cubans of days gone by. As we headed towards the port area, Juanita said she had something exciting to show us. It turned out to be a cigar shop. According to Juanita, it was the best one in the whole of Cuba.

The small store was dingy and stank of smoke and matches, but it did have an extensive range of cigars. I bought some of the huge Winston Churchill for my dad, my sons, and me. Of course, I wouldn't be able to tell my family they were Winston Churchill cigars. That would set off my father, who hated the Tories, and Churchill in particular. Something to do with him ordering the army to break up a strike of Liverpool dockers in 1911. My dad, an ex-docker, and his former colleagues were an unforgiving bunch with long memories.

After the grizzly old shop owner wrapped up the cigars for me, I took another gander around the place and noticed bottles of rum available for the equivalent of two pound.

Though tempted to buy a bottle, I knew there'd be other opportunities.

In the next square, Sally approached Juanita. "Is there anywhere you'd recommend eating? An excellent restaurant?" She enunciated her words more than was necessary and raised her voice in both octave and volume. Once again, I cringed.

"Why yes, Havana has many fine paladars."

"Paladars?" Sally squinted in confusion. I was about to explain, but Juanita got in before me.

"Privately run restaurants in Cuba."

I'd read in a newspaper back home before our trip, that paladars were relatively new in Cuba. They'd sprung up after Raúl Castro finally persuaded his brother to let him play at president (at least that's the way I interpreted the situation between the brothers). This represented a step towards freeing and liberalising the economy and a move away from the stranglehold of the government on all aspects of Cuban life. There were also state-run restaurants, palamars.

"A restaurant then?" Sally asked. Juanita nodded. "Is here, on this square, a good place?"

"Yes, there is a great paladar there." Juanita pointed to a decrepit building.

Sally looked sceptical. I agreed with her sentiment. "You would recommend that place?" Sally asked.

"Yes, of course."

"Could you book us a table for tonight? Say seven?"

At that, Juanita went off and disappeared into the building. She reappeared five minutes later. "Booked for seven on the terrace. One of Havana's best restaurants."

"Thank you, that's lovely, thank you very much." Sally turned to me and squealed.

"How exciting." I grinned.

She squeezed my arm. "Can't wait."

I could only hope it lived up to the hype.

By the time we got to the Plaza de Armas, in Old Havana, one of the last stops on our tour, my feet throbbed, and I needed some time out. The sun was baking hot in a cloudless sky. Thankfully, Juanita read my thoughts, or my body language, and guided us to a shady area, where she delivered a quick talk on the local history then told us to take a brief break.

In the square, a book market was taking place. Set out on numerous tables were books, art prints, memorabilia, and magazines and newspapers dating back to the 1940s. I'd always loved books but had sold most of them a few years before to help fund a trip to Disney World with a former girlfriend and her family. It wasn't exactly the lover's jaunt I'd hoped it would be. A story for another time.

The books reminded me of who I used to be, and a momentary melancholy washed over me. Years earlier, I would read a couple of books a week. Science fiction was a staple in my reading diet, along with history, politics, and current affairs. But I'd lost my appetite after my divorce when I lost myself amongst the battles.

Thankfully, the activity of the present moment quickly dispelled my nostalgia. The plaza was surrounded by pastel-coloured buildings, and in the centre was a disused fountain. Sea salt wafted on the air from the Atlantic Ocean, within walking distance, along with the savoury scent of roast chicken from a nearby outdoor restaurant. Various tour groups congregated in the shaded parts of the square, and their shouts mingled with those of the sellers approaching them. The place bustled, and pushy sellers bristled with keenness to show off their wares and make a sale.

Sally was in shopping heaven—her first chance to browse. I kept a beady eye on her to make sure she didn't antagonise the locals. I'd seen her make grown men cry with her haggling tactics.

While I sat in the shade to rest for a moment, my gaze landed on a young dog laid flat out, a dozen strides away, in the sun's direct glare, not moving or breathing. No one paid the poor dead dog any attention. Sally joined me and pointed at the canine cadaver. "I can't believe everyone is just walking by. How can they do that?" A tear ran down her cheek.

I was immediately distraught. Sally's moods had that effect on me—if she was sad, I was inconsolable; if she was happy, I was ecstatic. I'd always been empathetic, and my emotion detector could run strong. "What type of people wander past a dead dog?" I blurted loudly. "Where is their compassion?" People carried on, now ignoring both the creature and me. I stood and gestured to the prostrate pooch. "This is outrageous. Why doesn't someone move the dead animal?"

Minutes went by, and I took to giving everyone who walked past the motionless mutt an evil look. "That's right, just walk past the dead dog."

Sally gripped my arm and looked mournfully into my eyes. "Baby, will you move it? It's distressing me, seeing it lying there."

As strongly as I felt about the issue, my indignation didn't stretch to touching or moving it. "What, me? But where do I put it? And what about fleas or rabies?"

"Please?" Her face drooped further into sadness, her eyes large and pleading.

How could I say no? Even though the thought of picking it up made me retch and itch, I walked towards the dog. Within touching distance, I crouched, and as I stretched out my hand, the mendacious mongrel sprang Lazarus-like to life, gave me a cursory look, and wandered over to a cooler spot to resume its death-like slumber.

I took that as my cue. Time for my siesta. We had a big evening ahead.

8
WHERE'S DINNER?

While Sally had enjoyed the tour and things seemed to be looking up, I was eager for the opportunity to wine and dine her and solidify my place in her life.

A taxi dropped us off at the place Juanita had booked for us, and we climbed one set of stairs and then another until we finally reached a rooftop terrace. Out of breath, my legs weak, I followed a waiter to our table and my heart sunk a little. The terrace was empty. And quiet, too. No music. Nothing. I hoped we wouldn't be the only customers for long.

The lighting was dim and romantic, but the effect was somewhat spoilt by the hotchpotch of chairs and tables. As I sat down, I inspected the white tablecloth and spotted a red-wine stain. At least I hoped it was wine and not the alternative.

I mustered a smile for Sally, who sat opposite me at the small table for two near the edge of the terrace. A disgruntled waiter approached. Without a word or a glimmer of warmth, he looked at us, a notepad and pencil at the ready. A monobrow worthy of a Mancunian rock star and deep-set eyes gave him a rather menacing appearance.

I glanced at Sally and lifted my shoulders; she returned the gesture.

"Hi," I said to the waiter. "Good evening. How are you this beautiful night?"

"What do you want to eat?"

I picked up a menu. "We're still looking, but in the meantime"—I turned to Sally—"shall we share a bottle of red wine?"

She placed her hand on top of mine and smiled. "Yes, that would be lovely."

I grinned and then stared up at the waiter again. His off-white shirt was creased. "Yes, a bottle of red wine, please."

"No."

My eyes widened. "No red wine?"

"Not possible." He stared up at the night sky.

"Any red wine?" I pleaded.

"No. Not possible."

"How come no red wine?" Sally asked.

"I tell you. NO red wine. NOT possible."

Sally and I exchanged confused glances. "What do you reckon?" I asked her. "A bottle of white?"

Sally folded her arms with a grunt. "Okay, white wine, then."

I smiled at the waiter. "A bottle of white wine, please?"

He wrote on his pad. Progress.

"What do you want to eat?" He picked up another menu and tossed it at Sally.

I leant forward. "You chosen yet?"

Silly question. She'd been holding the menu for less than five seconds.

She shook her head and pouted.

I peeked up at him. "We're still looking. Bring us the wine and we'll let you know."

He tutted and stomped off.

"How rude," Sally hissed. "There's no need for that kind of behaviour at all. What's his problem?"

"I know. Strange." I scanned the terrace. "So empty here."

Was this Juanita's way of getting revenge for what she probably considered Sally's impertinent and persistent questioning earlier in the day? Before I had time to dive into that unpleasant thought, I glanced down at the road to see a coach pull up and a swarm of elderly tourists disembark. A couple of bags displayed the flag of Canada. They piled into the establishment, and within minutes, every table on the terrace was full. Was this the same crowd from breakfast? Were they following us? Was it our fate to be followed at every turn by loud Canadian tourists?

The world's worst waiter returned with a bottle of red wine. I said nothing, only smiled. He turned to walk away.

"May I have the Wi-Fi code for the restaurant?" Sally asked.

He spun around, his face like thunder. "No. Not possible." He stormed off. I took this to mean he might or might not arrive minutes later with a Wi-Fi code.

Sally huffed, took out her phone, fiddled with it, and put it back in her bag while I poured out our wine. The waiter returned, spied our full glasses, shook his head, and muttered to himself. He half-turned.

I held up my hand. "Excuse me. Can we order now?"

"No. I'll come back." He strode away to the kitchen.

Sally glanced around. "Every other table is getting bread and jugs of water. Where's ours?"

I tried to find our man, but he was missing in action.

Forty-five minutes after our arrival, we'd not had even a sniff of food. I poured the last of the wine into our glasses. My plans for a romantic evening were in serious peril. There was a rumbling in my belly, either hunger or nerves about Sally's likely reaction to the unfolding events.

A waiter serving the next table smiled at us. I waved at him, and he approached.

"Excuse me. Some bread and water, please."

He bowed and smiled. "The bread is being baked specially for you."

I frowned. That had to be a lie.

Sally snorted. "Is that true? We were here first and everybody but us has bread."

Uh-oh, here we go.

He bowed again. "Please, I'll check."

She patted her forehead with her napkin. "I'm starving. I'm going to faint."

The waiter returned five minutes later with a lump of cold, stale bread.

I smiled grimly. "Well, this is lovely. Rooftop terrace in Havana." I picked up my glass of wine. "To us." Sally held up her glass with a disinterested look on her face. "Cheers." We drained the last of the wine.

"I'm starving," she repeated. "Where's our waiter?" She stared down at her watch and tapped her fingers on the table. "And I want more wine. Anything to take the edge off."

Spotting him at a nearby table, I gestured to him and shouted, "Excuse me!" He came back.

"What do you want to eat?"

"Another bottle of wine, please. Red if you have." I tapped the top of the empty bottle hopefully.

"The soup to start and lobster for the main course, please," Sally said.

"Same," I said. "Soup to start and fillet steak for the main course."

"No lobster and no fillet steak."

"Oh," Sally said. "Well, the prawns then."

"Sirloin steak for me."

He snatched the menus and left again. If this was the best Havana had to offer, we were in big trouble. Sally stared out at the port area, which was behind me, looking miserable. Desperate, my mind grasped at ways to improve our evening, to lighten the mood, to start up a sparkling conversation. So far, the conversation had been limited to snarky comments about the state of the restaurant and the noise levels of the other customers. Inspiration eluded me. "What did you think of the tour today?" I ventured.

She rapped her fingers on her wineglass then downed its contents. I picked up the bottle and poured air into her glass, forgetting it was bereft of wine. She swigged back a couple of droplets of wine, smiled weakly and checked her watch. "I don't know. It was okay. Where's our soup?"

I glugged back my wine. "Not sure."

She leant back. "Are you going to sit there and do nothing?"

Why was it always on me? I wiggled in my seat. "Well, no, I'll find out."

Just then, a waiter dropped off two bowls of soup, a bottle of white wine, and our main courses. Sally stared at me with ferocity in her gaze.

"Sorry," I said to the waiter. "There's been a mistake. We ordered the soup as a starter, not to come with our main course."

"Sorry?" he said, looking confused.

Our angry friend turned up and spoke to the other waiter in Spanish. Then he stormed off after saying, "No, no, they can eat it together." The waiter just shrugged and walked away.

I looked at our plates, which both appeared to hold some kind of beef dish with rice and salad. Not the dishes we'd ordered. My body tensed and anger bubbled away in my gut. I put my hand up.

"Put your hand down," Sally hissed. "You're not at school."

"But they've brought the wrong dishes."

"Leave it. At this point, I'd eat one of your socks."

Desperate talk from Sally, as they stunk to high heaven.

The beef dish was as salty as the Dead Sea. My mouth dried up immediately. I needed water. Once again, our man was nowhere to be seen. I flagged down another staff member. "Excuse me, some water, please?"

No water came. Ten minutes later, another member of staff came by. "Excuse me, some water, please?"

Time ebbed away, along with our wine. No water came.

"Let's just go," Sally said. "This has been an unmitigated disaster of an evening. I want to go back to the hotel, drink some mojitos, and access some Wi-Fi."

I nodded. The evening had indeed been a bust, and I had no desire to draw it out. With no sign of our guy, I checked a menu, worked out the bill, and left several notes on the table.

As I walked away, Sally counted the money. "Hang on—did you leave money for a tip?"

"Yeah, but a nominal one."

"You think he deserves extra money?"

"No, but I always leave one."

"No. Not tonight." With that, she grabbed one note, stuck it in her bag, and stared me down as she thundered past. I chased after her. As we approached the stairs, a man, the restaurant owner, perhaps, who was laughing and joking with the chef, barred our escape.

"Good evening. How did you enjoy your meal?" He rubbed his hands together and bowed slightly. Then he smiled smarmily.

A red rag in front of the bull that was Sally. She wagged her finger in his face and unleashed a verbal attack. "This was the worst restaurant I've ever been to in my life. The service was atrocious, the food disgusting, the wine tasted like petrol, and—"

"We're leaving," I finished. I took Sally's hand and tried to manoeuvre around the owner. As I did, our waiter jumped in front of us, waving the bill in my face. "More money. Not enough."

I snatched the bill. We owed an additional six bucks. For the *bread*.

Sally yanked a note out of her bag, threw it at the waiter, and stamped her way down the stairs, one at a time. "Take me back to the hotel. NOW."

It seemed pretty clear to me now: Juanita, like Dawn, was a vengeful woman not to be messed with.

9
WORLD'S SHORTEST TAXI RIDE

The next morning, the cockroach and his mate didn't turn up to wave us off; a blessing for them but mostly for me. My pride had taken enough of a battering after the events at the paladar. According to Sally, it was the worst restaurant she'd ever been to, and I was the worst boyfriend ever. Not for the first time, my feelings of inadequacy threatened to spiral out of control.

A voice in my head berated me for all my inadequacies, causing a headache and nausea (though this could also have been a side effect of the cheap wine). At least we had the distraction of a travel day ahead. I hoped that would lift me out of my mood, which had swung deep and low.

We were off to Cienfuegos. Afterwards, we'd travel on to Trinidad (the Cuban one, not the more-famous Caribbean one) and Varadero. Then, after a quick detour to the Cayman Islands, we'd return to Havana on New Year's Eve. I'd wanted to take in Santa Clara because of its connection to Che Guevara—the city had a museum and statues dedicated to him—but Sally overruled me on that one. Something to do with overdosing on communism. Unlike me, she didn't have a left-wing past and would have been more interested in visiting the birthplace of Nigel Farage, the UKIP leader.

Our first job of the day was to get seats on a coach from Havana to Cienfuegos. We arrived at the station via taxi. My excitement overcame the negative feelings I'd woken up with, my headache and nausea eased, and I even felt bright-eyed and bushy-tailed, full of optimism and adventure. I hadn't been able to book tickets in advance for the tourist buses that traverse Cuba, the Viazul, as the website had kept crashing, but I'd read that if I arrived at the coach station early, I could purchase tickets there and jump on the first bus out.

First, though, we had to navigate the many taxi drivers gathered outside the coach station's entrance. I gave each of them a stern no and held my hand out while shaking my head. A coach seemed safer to me. I'd dissuade one driver only for another to approach, offering me a ride to wherever I needed to go.

Finally, we managed to enter the building. Inside the gloomy, concrete space was a desk and a queue that appeared to be full of locals. Naturally, I joined it. When my time came, I approached the desk with confidence and swagger. "Dos tickets to Cienfuegos, por favor."

The bloke behind the counter stared down at a newspaper looking as unimpressed as anyone could look. He said no and something in Spanish I didn't understand then pointed a bony finger in a vague direction.

I glanced at Sally, who stood by the back wall tapping her foot and tried to appear calm and collected. Meanwhile, my mind raced. Where the hell was the guy pointing? It appeared to be a wall on the other side of the coach station. Then he dismissed me with a jerk of his head, nodding in the direction he'd pointed.

"Everything is fine," I said, joining Sally, and we headed in the direction he'd pointed to find ourselves in a place to leave luggage. No one was there. We noticed another door. I opened it with trepidation, fearing it was the staff toilet, but was happily surprised to find it led to a larger, cleaner, and more salubrious concourse full of tourists with cases and backpacks. Success!

Sally sauntered over to a seat and stared at her phone. I wandered around. There were no signs but plenty of unhelpful employees. I found another queue and, as would be expected of any Brit, joined at the back, praying it was the ticket line. When I eventually got to the front, the staff member left their booth and sauntered off. On their return minutes later, I asked for two tickets.

"No! You go there!" He pointed towards a longer queue, at the other end of the hall, and informed me I was at the check-in desk and needed to purchase a coach ticket first.

I knew I should have asked someone in the queue, but talking to strangers, especially in a country where many don't speak English, caused me anxiety. My shoulders slumped as my stress levels rose, and with my tail between my legs, I joined another line of weary travellers.

Sally spotted me, held up her arms, and mouthed, "What the hell?"

I grimaced and turned my back. Given that I couldn't comprehend what the hell was going on, I had no energy to try to explain it to her. *Please let this be the right line.*

Eventually, I progressed to the front of the line and spoke to a heavily made-up woman wearing the usual Benny Hill uniform that all working Cuban women appeared to be forced to wear. The best news: I was in the right place.

I purchased two tickets, and she instructed me to join the check-in queue forty-five minutes before the coach left. I did so, straight away, as a precautionary measure, as the coach was due to leave in an hour. When I got to the front, the attendant informed me I didn't need to be there as I'd purchased a ticket. For fuck's sake. I wanted to scream. He told me to join the luggage queue—one of the very first lines I'd joined.

In this small queue were other bemused-looking tourists. They appeared to love their bureaucracy, the Cubans. I hated it; it jarred against my desire for order and simplicity.

Time ticked by with no sign of anyone. Finally, a Cuban official sauntered over and told us that he wouldn't be checking in luggage and to put the bags on the coach ourselves. A murderous rage overcame me, but I resisted. I'd probably need to join another queue for murderous rages.

Wandering outside to catch the coach, I had high expectations of the Viazul, despite its clunky website that kept crashing and provided little information and few pictures. But I assumed that as it was primarily for foreigners, the coaches would be of a high standard, with air conditioning, luxury toilets, and the latest videos streaming on individual screens for us.

"Is that it?" Sally pointed at a world-weary bus.

"Of course not," I replied optimistically. "That'll be for the locals. We're travelling first class." But my stomach did a flip. A sliver of doubt forced its way into my brain. *Four and a half hours on that.*

"Thank God for that."

An announcement blared in Spanish, invoking a flurry of activity. People around us gathered their belongings.

Surely not.

The frenzy intensified, and further instructions were barked out in Spanish. "Excuse me," Sally asked two tall blond men as they started moving toward the old bus. "Is that the coach to Cienfuegos?"

"Yes. The bus to Cienfuegos. Are you going there?"

"Yes," Sally said, fluttering her eyelashes. "Yes, we are."

"Hurry then."

"I'll definitely hurry for you, darling." She cocked her head and smiled at him.

I stared at Sally and shook my head. The man grimaced and spoke to his friend in a language I didn't understand. Given that I only comprehend English, that didn't narrow down my guesses much. My curiosity about their accents trumped my shyness and usual unwillingness to engage with strangers. "We're from the UK," I said. "How about you?"

"Sweden."

They both had piercing blue eyes and a handsome ruggedness about them. I could see why Sally was enamoured of them. I sighed. "Come on, Sally, this is our transport to Cienfuegos. I'm sure the inside is much better than the outside," I said, much less optimistically than before. *I bet it's a shithole, like the exterior.*

Correct. The interior was atrocious. The toilet didn't work and blocked up within half an hour of departure. When the air conditioning switched on it sounded like a chainsaw, and after five minutes, the roof deposited enormous droplets of water into the coach. Luckily, the drops hit only one of us irregularly. The fundamental problem was solved when I swapped places with Sally. At least I got to rescue her, which warmed my heart a little. Everything about the coach screamed mid-eighties. Oh, and the seats were covered in long hair. I wondered whether cats had been fighting in the bus. I hoped it wasn't something more gruesome than that.

But the coach's atrocity paled in comparison to that of its driver. He spent more time texting and talking on a brick-like mobile than paying attention to the road. I felt a sharp poke in my ribs.

"Has he got any hands on the wheel?"

I rubbed my side and examined him. As he talked quickly and loudly, he gesticulated wildly. He had no hands on the steering wheel, and we were rapidly approaching a tight bend in the road.

I closed my eyes. Panic-stricken, I waited for the inevitable. Hearing no crunching of metal or screaming, I peeked through my eyelids and saw he now had one hand on the wheel. *Thank God for small mercies.*

The bus stopped in a nondescript village with no announcement. No one got off except the driver and another Viazul employee. They disappeared and returned with several people carrying bags of food. Perhaps to sell to the passengers? Wrong. They scoffed the lot all by themselves. This happened a couple more times.

Thankfully, an hour and a half into our trip, we were allowed off the bus at a service station to eat. Given the state of the coach, my expectations were rock-bottom low. But the stop turned out to be the highlight of the trip. We were greeted by a chef armed with a prong and a massive knife, with which he sliced through roast pork. The meat was placed on warm, soft buns. The food tasted as delicious as it looked. The most luxurious pit stop ever. I wanted to find out which communist bureaucrat was responsible, as this person would end up either being a leader or locked up sharpish for an inspired and dangerous concession to capitalism.

Just when I was thinking our luck had changed, the bus broke down midway between Havana and Cienfuegos, and the driver banged on pipes for a good forty-five minutes, providing no explanation or timeline. Locals gathered, sensing the opportunity for excitement or money or both. One by one, fellow tourists peeled away and into waiting cars. Not wanting to be left out, Sally and I quickly agreed to pay a local to drive us the rest of the way. No reservations required on this occasion. Wondering afterwards, I contemplated the possibility, the breakdown, was a ruse, to earn some locals extra tourist dollars.

I brightened. This would be a fantastic way to talk to a Cuban and ask them about the country, communism, and Fidel.

Once we were settled in a car, I turned to the driver. "So, do you enjoy living in Cuba?"

He stared ahead. "Yes."

"How do you feel about communism?"

He shook his head. "No."

"Was Fidel an outstanding leader?"

He nodded. "Yes."

"Do you like his brother?"

"No." He wound down his window and spat out of it.

The scintillating conversation ended, and two hours later, he dropped us off at the bus station in Cienfuegos.

Sally and I stepped out of the vehicle to receive a warm welcome in the form of hot air blasting us in the face. Glancing around, I immediately thought of a Wild West town: dusty roads and wind blowing that dust around. I didn't spy any cowboys, but maybe that would come later.

I kept an eye out for a person carrying a sign with our names on it but couldn't spot one. I'd asked for a transfer to our casa particular. Essentially Cuban B&Bs, casa particulars were privately run—part of Cuba's subtle economic liberalisation.

With a sinking feeling, I remembered I hadn't received a reply from the owner of the home. An emerging pattern. Did our host even know about our arrival? My nerves kicked up a notch. I had an invoice and confirmation email printed off, but the documents were from the third-party hosting site. Did we have a place to sleep tonight?

I took a deep breath. I'd come on this trip to stop Sally from dumping me, but all the signs pointed to the conclusion that I'd be unceremoniously dumped anyway. The atmosphere between us had been tepid all day. She'd been silent, which was most unlike her. And there was only one thing worse than a vocally angry Sally: a quiet Sally.

The coach station's forecourt was a cacophony of noise, and we quickly found ourselves surrounded by locals trying to sell us rooms and taxis. Sally stared at me, seemingly looking for reassurance. "Babe, what's happening?"

I don't have a clue. "Need to sort out a taxi to our place." I put a hand on her arm and kept my feet around our bags.

She shrugged off my hand. "You said they'd meet us here."

I faced her and summoned my confidence. "No, we need to do it ourselves."

She waved me away. "For God's sake, I can't rely on you for anything." Sally shoved her way through the throng and approached a handsome Cuban man in his early twenties. I gathered up all our baggage and followed her.

I heard her say, "Oh, you'll do." She giggled as she stroked his bicep and squeezed it. Then she turned to me with a scowl. "What's the address?"

I held out the piece of paper, and the man snatched it from my hand, read the contents, and said, "Follow me."

I grabbed Sally's arm. "Babe, we don't know this man and whether he's a taxi driver."

"Who cares—have you seen the muscles on him?" She giggled again.

She was having another Luther moment, except this time with a real man, right in front of me. A sharp pain stabbed me in my solar plexus, but I suppressed the jealousy. I couldn't afford it right now. This trip was about making Sally happy, and at least she was talking again.

"Wait," I called out. "Please. How much?"

"Don't be silly," Sally whispered. "He'll be worth the cost."

I gawped at Sally, the same woman who'd reduced a stall-holder in Marrakesh to tears with her tough negotiation techniques.

"Five bucks," the driver said.

Here was an opportunity to impress Sally. I shook my head. "No. Too much."

He checked his watch. "How much you pay?"

"One dollar." He walked away. "Wait." He turned around. "Two." My eyes pleaded with him to accept.

He observed the scene around him and turned to me. "Three bucks. No less."

"Okay, three bucks." I smiled and winked at Sally, seeking affirmation for my brilliance. I'd negotiated a 40 per cent reduction in the price.

Sally shook her head. "What was all that about? These people are poor. We could have afforded five bucks." She stated loudly, for the driver's benefit.

I threw my arms in the air. "You always negotiate down. What's different this time?"

"Oh, don't start," she said, placing her hands on her hips. "I can see you're getting all jealous and trying to make a point."

Sometimes I couldn't win with her. As the smile on my face faded, the one on the taxi drivers bloomed. He appeared delighted with the deal, and that made me even less happy about it. He grabbed our bags, making it look easy.

We followed him in silence. Sally got into the back of his car. The driver shoved our bags into the boot. Then, as I was about to clamber into the front seat, the driver pulled on my arm and said quietly, "You want to keep a close eye on her." He pointed at his eye and then at Sally.

"What do you mean?"

"A woman like that who flirts with another man in front of her husband . . . No, you cannot trust." He went around to his side and climbed in.

I sat down in the car, frowning. Sally flirted with loads of men. It meant nothing—she'd made that clear from the beginning. Harmless fun. Sure, it sometimes made me uncomfortable, but I didn't want to make a thing of it and upset her. She got jealous when I talked to other women, but that wasn't the same. There were different dynamics involved. I think?

She touched my shoulder, breaking my train of thought. I turned around. She held her palm to the left side of her mouth, shielding it from the driver. "What did he say?" she whispered.

I contemplated the driver, half-covered my mouth, and whispered, "Wondering if we wanted a taxi back. I said no. I know you don't like to operate by timetables and schedules."

She leant back into her seat and stared at the driver, trying to catch his eye in the rear-view mirror. "I'd make an exception for him."

Again, came that gnawing insecurity. My mood soured.

The man drove out of the coach station. Two streets down, he turned left. Then one hundred metres down the road, he stopped. I thought the car had conked out, but he got out, went up to a house, and knocked on the door. A woman who appeared to be in her early thirties answered, and he came back to the car and unloaded our backpacks. The entire drive had lasted less than a minute—negotiations had taken longer than the actual journey itself.

Thieving little git, I thought, as I paid up.

10

HEALTH AND SAFETY?

"Kelly. Yari," the woman said, pointing at herself. She gestured us inside the house.

"Kevin. Sally." I pointed as well.

"Kelly." She beckoned me up a flight of stairs. When she reached the top, she turned and peeked down at me. I was several steps behind, maintaining a dignified distance and avoiding staring at her backside. "*Español?*"

"No." I shook my head. "English?"

Yari shook her head. My stomach twisted, and I froze to the spot. How the hell were we supposed to communicate? While planning for the holiday, I'd assumed that the locals would know English. But I'd been presented with enough examples now to realise this wasn't the case. The locals speaking English was the exception, not the rule.

Sally tugged at my elbow. "Babe, what's happening. Why aren't you moving?"

"Nothing. I'm trying to think."

"About what? Let's go to our room." She nodded towards the top of the stairs.

At the top, Yari opened a door, and we were outside, on a

walkway, attached to the back of the house, with rooms, on the left-hand side and a railing on the right-hand side.

Yari halted. "Kelly." Yari beckoned and smiled, saying something to us in Spanish. I turned to Sally, who shrugged. Yari held up a finger and nodded. Then she made fists and alternated moving them towards her mouth.

"Aha! Dinner. What time do you want food, Sal?"

"Hmm, seven?"

I held up seven fingers then approached Yari and gripped her wrist lightly. On her watch, I started at the seven and traced my finger to the twelve.

Yari nodded and shook her finger in the air. She made a fist, pulled it towards her slightly open mouth, made a slurping noise, and gulped.

"What do you reckon?" I asked Sally, who just shook her head. Yari repeated the actions. Realisation dawned. "Aha. Soup. She means soup."

"How lovely, darling. Ask her what soup it is."

I glared at Sally. "Really?" I faced Yari and nodded. "Okay, no, yes, we will have soup."

She held her clenched fists up to her ample breasts and flapped her arms. The motion mesmerised me. Next, she made clucking noises.

"Chicken. Yes. Sí. Sí." I nodded for good measure.

Yari took my hand, walked me towards the end of the walkway, and pointed to a gate and some stairs that led upwards. She held up seven fingers.

I nodded. Yari led us back to our room. She pushed the door open, and Sally strode past her and in, leaving her bags outside. I heaved them in. When had I become her servant? Who was I kidding—I couldn't remember a time where I didn't carry her suitcases, or drive her everywhere, or cook all the meals. I was starting to resent it, but I had no choice but to continue as I always had if I wanted to avoid a huge argument.

At least we'd arrived safely at our home for the next couple of days. I spotted the bed. Feeling a rush of childlike enthusiasm, I jumped backwards and rolled into the middle.

"OW! OUCH. What the—"

Surrounding the centre, which had no springs, was metal that dug in firmly but not enough to stop a body from rolling. From the bed, I caught sight of a tiny en-suite bathroom with a green sink and toilet circa 1970. The tiles were yellowy white, and the exposed walls were also painted green. The shower comprised a bulbous white showerhead attached with red tape to a greening copper pipe that jutted out of a hole in the tiling. Taped and tacked along the shower's length was various electrical wiring that disappeared into the showerhead. A health and safety inspector's worst nightmare. I considered asking Sally to test it but knew, in my heart of hearts, that I would be the one to conduct the trial run.

I got up, closed my eyes, and pressed the switch. No jolts of electricity ran through me, and within seconds warm water pumped out of the showerhead. Switching it off, I breathed out, my test complete. Even so, I hoped Sally would be the one to take the first shower and test it properly.

I returned to the bedroom to continue my inspection. On the wall hung one picture. Out of curiosity, I lifted it and discovered a gaping hole in the plaster that allowed me a view of the outside. I shifted it back into place. No point crying over cavernous holes in the wall, dangerous showers, and a mattress with life-ending metal springs. This was home sweet home for the next few days.

"Shall we go out and explore for a bit?" Sally said. "I want some fresh air."

Still averse to the idea of exploring on our own, I wondered if someone could drive us around the major highlights of the city, or town. It was supposed to be a city, but I was still convinced it had all the trappings of a Wild West town. "Yeah, let me see if I can get Yari to fix us up."

Sally pouted.

I picked up my guidebook. "It'll be great—give me one minute." I left the room and headed to the landing outside. "Yari. YARI."

She appeared in a doorway at the top of the stairs, which I assumed led to her house. She beamed. Her smile was infectious. I moved toward her, found the section on Cienfuegos in my guidebook, and pointed at the map. Next, I lowered my body into a seated position and placed my palm above my eyebrow, peering around and pretending to talk to an imaginary person next to me.

Yari nodded and grabbed my arm. "Sí. Sí."

She disappeared, and I returned to the room.

"What's happening, darling? I need to get out of here. I've not come away to sit in a room that could feature on a home makeover programme, this being the before room." She gingerly sat on the bed, avoiding the errant springs, arms folded tight across her chest.

I paced. "I'm sure Yari will be back soon."

As if by magic, there was a knock on the door. "Kelly. Kelly."

"See, I told you." I smiled and opened the door. Yari stood there grinning and gestured for me to follow her.

"Come on, love, we're off. Let's go."

Sally stood. "Don't hassle me. I need to fetch my phone and bag."

"Over there." I pointed at her bag, in the corner. "You won't need your mobile."

She snatched her bag, which was like a Tardis. I'd once witnessed her empty it—far more stuff came out than could physically fit in. She dug around and fished out her mobile. "For photos, and perhaps we'll find somewhere with Wi-Fi. Can't believe you booked a place without internet."

"Yes, but at least we can charge our phones here. That plug in the bathroom works for the charger."

"Yeah, whatever."

I followed Yari along the landing, down the stairs, and out into the street, where I stood open-mouthed and waited with dread for Sally and her reaction.

"Hey babe . . ." Sally trailed off as she spotted what I was staring at. "What the blazes is that?" She pointed across the road at the horse and cart waiting for us.

The wooden cart had clearly gone twelve rounds with a Roman chariot. Bare wood poked through various gaps in the paint. The seat was a plank complete with complementary splinters.

Yari was beaming with pride, and I didn't have the heart to refuse the tour she'd arranged for us. I moved closer to the horse, which seemed bigger than normal. Then again, I'd never seen one up close and personal. It was certainly bigger than the donkey I'd ridden in Blackpool years ago, which was the closest I'd come to riding a horse. I stroked it but withdrew my hand sharpish when it shook its mane.

The driver smiled, and I inwardly jumped back—he made my smile look positively American. His ears were elephantine, and he stared at me through dark eyes that sat in a skeletal face.

Yari introduced us. He held out his hand, and I gripped his sweaty palm and shook twice, but he continued to shake my hand and grin his toothy smile. Finally, he released my grip and helped us both into the open-top cart. I plonked myself on the bench, avoiding the splinters. Still, my bottom hurt immediately. Sally adopted the face of a mannequin, and her forced smile stayed fixed until there was some distance between our abode and us.

Our whistle-stop tour of the top attractions involved the

driver talking in Spanish and pointing and us nodding and saying "Look, it's a . . . yeah, what the hell is that?"

A few highlights:

A park with a white statue of a man holding his right arm out. At the bottom was another statue—a female gripping a shield in her left hand. Surrounding the ensemble was a small, ornate metal fence painted white.

An elegant-looking building that appeared to be an old-style music hall. *Teatro Tomás Terry* was displayed in big letters near the top, painted on a thin wooden board screwed to the building. I assumed *Teatro* meant *theatre*. Terry Thomas was a quintessential English actor in the 1950s who often played scoundrels. I wondered why they'd name a theatre after him. Maybe because Thomas played upper-class cads, the Cubans believed that he helped overthrow their upper-class bounders? Or perhaps there was another explanation that escaped me. I later read after the holiday, he was the Cuban *Rockefeller*, in his day, with Irish descent too.

A stadium. Baseball, perhaps? Our guide seemed excited about it, so I assumed that it was sports-related and he was a supporter of whoever played there. I'd read that Cubans' favourite sports included baseball, soccer, and volleyball. Too big to be a volleyball stadium, and too rounded for soccer, so baseball seemed to be the most likely answer.

An enormous building—a palace? —whose architecture reminded me of many buildings we saw in Marrakesh.

"Is he pointing at the beach?" Sally asked at one point. "Or that tree over there?"

"The sea?"

Then she pointed towards a dog. "Is he showing us that dog over there? Is it a famous one?"

"Perhaps the mutt is the reincarnation of Ernest Hemingway and the locals sit around the canine on an evening while he woofs his way through stories of love, lust, power, and adventure."

"I worry about you sometimes."

"Just sometimes?"

Sally giggled and moved closer to me.

I grinned. "Hang on, he's stopping the cart and pointing at that place there. Must be a famous local landmark. I wish I knew what it was. Looks like the other homes in this street, to be honest."

"That's because it's where we're staying, you idiot."

I leant forward and stared at the building. Yari appeared in the doorway. "Oh, yeah," I said, blushing. "So it is."

It might not have been the tour I'd expected, or that Sally had wanted, but it had lightened the mood and relaxed us both. We felt privileged to have been part of such a unique experience. Sally pecked me on the cheek before getting out of the cart, and I glowed inwardly and let out a deep sigh. Mission accomplished.

That balmy evening, we slurped tomato soup and feasted on chicken on the rooftop terrace. The food and drink cost extra, they were not included in the price for the accommodation. No worries about the additional cost, as I was sure it was cheaper than a restaurant. I'd surreptitiously slipped a blue pill into my mouth half an hour earlier. I'd never told Sally about my need for a little chemical help before our love making—my very own little secret from her. No need to undermine her confidence in me, and to be honest, I worried enormously about the ramifications of telling her eighteen months into our relationship. I imagined a massive argument in which she accused me of being deceitful before dumping me. Again.

Once we'd finished eating, I turned to Sally. "Shall we retire for the evening?" Then I winked. I hoped it came across as flirtatious rather than terrifying. I'd never mastered the art of winking flirtatiously.

She smiled and squeezed my hand.

Was this evening about to have a perfect ending? Excitement bubbled in my belly for a change. Then came the trepidation. Would the pill work? Would I work? Would we work together? I kept hold of her hand and stood, pulling her along. We passed Yari on the way. With my other hand, I gave her a thumbs up and pointed towards the table. It had been a delicious meal. Everything was coming up roses.

Back in our room, I pulled Sally towards me and kissed her passionately. As her knees buckled, I grabbed her around the waist and held her closer. The chemistry between us at the beginning of our relationship had been excellent. It was still great when things were good between us. A stirring told me the tablet and the kissing were having the desired effect. I nibbled her ear and kissed her neck to the sounds of appreciative oohs and aahs. My excitement grew. Our intimate life had cooled somewhat in recent months, and now I had an opportunity to relight the fire.

I kicked the door shut. "Get in bed!"

Sally fluttered her eyelashes and squeezed my bicep. "Look at you, being all masterful." She skipped to the bed, undressing as she did. Just before she disappeared under the covers, she flung off her underwear.

And then I doubled over. A cramp in my belly suddenly gripped me and wormed its way downwards. I clenched my buttocks tight to avoid flatulence spoiling the mood. For the love of God, what the hell was happening to my body and why now? Hopefully, it would pass. Maybe it was just a bit of wind I could surreptitiously release.

She patted the bed. "Come on then, handsome." She knew I loved it when she called me that.

Feeling better again, I exhaled with relief and sauntered round to my side of the bed, trying to increase the sexual tension and add to the mood of anticipation. I slowly unbuttoned my shirt before peeling it off my body. Then another cramp struck me, low down in my belly, and it took all my strength to avoid blowing off right there and then. I screwed up my face. A release now would be far from surreptitious.

"You okay, darling?" Sally furrowed her brow. "I hope you realise that wasn't a sexy look." She patted the bed again.

"Yep, I'm fine," I spat out between gritted teeth as my belly tightened and spasmed again. A barely audible bottom burp exited my body. I took a deep breath. The pain was making me sweat.

"Now whip off your jeans." Sally giggled.

Trying to gaze seductively at her as another cramp made its way through my body, I slowly unbuttoned my jeans and pulled the zip down. Then I bent forward and farted. Loudly.

Crap.

"Just give me a couple of minutes," I said breathlessly. Without waiting for her reaction, I twirled around, scurried to the bathroom, and pulled down my underpants just in time. The evacuation began before my cheeks touched the seat. The process was thunderous and messy and painful. Nausea swept over me as it went on and on.

"You okay, darling? What's going on? Flipping heck, is that smell you?"

I heard her dry heave.

Eventually, it was finished. I took a few swift, deep breaths and dealt with the aftermath. Hot, sweaty, and mucky, I jumped in the dangerous shower and gingerly switched it on. Soon, scalding water arrived. I spent ages soaping myself down.

Despite my dehydration, I exited the bathroom determined to continue my sexy striptease.

"Hey, baby," I said, about to whip off my towel. I paused. Sally had her back to me. I sighed as I heard a low snore. I'd lost my chance.

Probably for the best. I couldn't imagine feeling less sexy.

11

SEAFOOD ADVENTURES

"Ow. Ouch. What the . . . hell."

Sally was snoring like a hog snuffling for truffles, and I wanted her awake to share in my misery.

I rolled myself from the middle of the bed back to my side—the opposite side I usually slept on. I'd ungraciously given my usual side to Sally in the middle of the night, as it was slightly more comfortable. Partly out of love and partly to play out the role of the gallant gentleman. Or martyr. After the events of last night, I felt I had brownie (no pun intended) points to earn.

The pit of sunken bed springs continued to stab me. "Ow."

Woof. Woof. Woof. A local dog had woken up and was informing the world.

Cock-a-doodle-do. The cockerel joined in the chorus.

Tweet. Tweet. Tweet. Great, some birds.

The dog barked again. Clearly, it was the conductor of this orchestra. Or the CIA had trained the animals to disrupt the tourist industry by keeping tourists awake so they'd leave poor reviews of places. In the dim light and to the sound of the animals' song, I thought about the missing spark between

Sally and me. I groaned quietly. I'd almost captured it last night. Damn my bowel movements. *Time to shake things up.*

Knowing I wouldn't be able to sleep any longer, I got up and had another shower. When I came out, Sally was awake.

"What happened to you last night?" she said, as she started getting ready for the day.

I flipped through my guidebook. "I don't know. Probably something I ate. It all happened so quickly."

"Shame that, for you, anyway."

"There's always now."

"Mood gone, to be honest."

I couldn't blame her.

"Let's go to breakfast," she said.

I followed her to the terrace, where breakfast resembled a feast. First, a dish of fruit, which I didn't eat but Sally did, followed by a massive basket of lightly toasted bread accompanied by butter, jam, and honey so fresh it contained honeycombs. Next, a huge jug of freshly squeezed orange juice, stacks of pancakes, a jar of yoghurt, and plates of eggs, cheese, and ham.

Feeling as though I were about to explode, but in a good way—one that wouldn't involve hellish noises and collateral damage—I let out a deep breath. "I'm stuffed. That should keep me going all day."

Sally turned her face to the sun and closed her eyes. "Isn't it lovely up here? I could stay here all day."

"Really?" I looked around at the gorgeous view. I was tempted to agree, but a more adventurous side of me felt prompted to disagree when I spotted the sea and a promenade.

"Yeah." She picked up her phone. "Can you check with Yari about Wi-Fi?"

"Babe, there is none. There's more to life than getting on the internet." I swept my arms around, gesturing to the view she'd just been admiring.

"Unlike you, I want to keep in touch with my family."

Ow. "I do, and we'll do that when we get to that posh hotel in Varadero. There'll be Wi-Fi to your heart's content."

She leant towards me. "I need it, Kevin. NOW."

I held up my hands in surrender. "I can't magic it from nowhere. I want to explore today, see some of Cienfuegos."

"We saw it all yesterday: the dog, the tree, and that massive building," she said, listing the events on her fingers.

"There's more on the seafront, like a restaurant that Fidel ate in."

"You and your bloody commie obsessions," she said with a sneer. "Not exactly romantic, is it?"

"A walk along the promenade, hand in hand, exploring the local scenery. That could be romantic? And perhaps we'll find somewhere with internet."

She regarded me. "Okay, that sounds better. You promise we'll try to find some Wi-Fi?"

I nodded. I loved the internet as much as the next person, but her obsession with finding Wi-Fi was starting to concern me. What was so important for her to check when we were here in Cuba, together? Then again, perhaps her maternal instincts overrode everything, and she just wanted to make sure Harry was okay. "Yes, we'll go for a wander, hit the front, and explore."

She waggled her finger at me. "You won't get us lost, will you? Remember what happened in Marrakesh."

I shifted in my seat and averted my gaze. "No, we have the guidebook and a map. Plus, the streets go in blocks and lines."

"Yeah, but yesterday you didn't even recognise the front door."

She had me there.

"I'll take a photo of it."

"It's a deal. Let me tart myself up first."

"Yeah, you think I'd be seen out with you with your bed hair frizzing all over the place?"

"Har-har."

~

Our route to the sea took us through a poverty-stricken neighbourhood. There was rubbish everywhere among the broken buildings, roads, and pavements. What struck me was the lack of working automobiles. We occasionally spotted a horse-drawn cart, like the deathtrap in which we'd toured the city yesterday. None of this was what I'd had in mind when booking a place in Cienfuegos. It was a stark reminder of how privileged I'd become. While poverty existed back home, and I'd grown up in a poor neighbourhood, this felt different, both quantitatively and qualitatively.

But I also saw plenty of families sitting together outside enjoying each other's company. Family seemed more important here. Back home, it was all about money and careers. It made me question my priorities.

We came across some dilapidated yet ornate old buildings that appeared to be shops. I peeked into a couple of doorways, which revealed cavernous spaces occupied by young, hip-looking locals who appeared disinterested in everything other than the smattering of objects on their tables.

One shop sold paintings at overinflated prices for tourists like us. Sally dismissed it, along with all the others. Nothing sparkled enough for her to go on a shopping frenzy, which was fantastic for my wallet.

As we transitioned to the promenade, the houses seemed to be better maintained, as did the roads, which were no longer dusty and crumbling. I took Sally's hand and smiled at her. She squeezed my hand. I was reminded of her softness, her playfulness, her desire to take care of me. "This is the life," I said. "Not a care in the world, walking along the seashore, holding hands with my gorgeous girlfriend." I swung our arms back and forth.

She beamed. "Aw, you say the loveliest things, darling."

Sometimes, it was so easy to make her happy. Moments like these kept me going during our difficult times.

In the distance was a harbour filled with boats. No, not boats. Superyachts. I pointed them out. "That looks fabulous. Can you see the size of those yachts?"

Sally imitated a meerkat. "Oh yeah, wow, let's head in that direction. Wonder if they have Wi-Fi?"

My shoulders slumped. "This is romantic, isn't it, babe?" I said, hoping to distract her before she started obsessing about the internet again and ruined the moment. "Walking along, just the two of us."

"It is, darling."

Catching sight of something on the shore, I frowned. Realising it was a rotting pig carcass, I felt my stomach turn. "Eurgh, that's disgusting," I said, quickening my pace to pass it.

"What is it, though?" Sally said, glancing back over her shoulder.

"You don't want to know."

A little further along were the entrails of another animal interspersed with the sand.

"What the hell is that smell?" Sally asked.

"Cor blimey, that's a corker."

"Worse than last night." She giggled.

I wanted to laugh too, but the stench in the air was too distracting. Our romantic walk along the Malecón ended with us dropping each other's hands so we could cover our noses and cross the road.

Luckily, we soon found the restaurant I'd wanted to stop at —the one that Fidel Castro had eaten in on his victorious march to Havana. Unluckily, we soon found that it might have been the first place an assassination attempt took place. The food was rank and murderous. The first sign something was amiss occurred when we sat down at the table and the server cleared away all the plates, cutlery, and cloth napkins. "Excuse me, may we have the napkins please?" I asked.

"No napkins."

"What about—"

The woman straightened and eyeballed me. "No napkins." They must have been for show?

Sally ordered fish and rice. I ordered chicken and rice. When the dishes arrived, Sally took one bite and scowled. "Yuk. Disgusting."

"That looks dark for fish," I said, raising an eyebrow. "What is it?"

She chewed noticeably. "Don't know, but it's very chewy."

I waved at the waitress. "Excuse me. May we have a bottle of water, please? And what fish is this?"

She stomped over and looked at Sally's plate. "Fish. Ray."

Ray? Surely not. "What, stingray?"

"Yes."

I held my hand over the plate. "Babe, don't eat any more of that."

"I'm not." She shoved the dish to one side.

The server brought two glasses of water. I shook my head. "Hi, yes, I asked for bottled water, please."

"No bottles." She walked away.

"Oh my goodness," Sally said with a giggle. "This is worse than that paladar the other night."

"I didn't quite imagine death by food poisoning as part of the adventure," I said with a chuckle. "Let's walk to those luxury boats and find a beautiful place to drink mojitos and relax."

As we left the restaurant, a yellow cab slowed down. "Where you go?" the driver asked.

"We're fine, thank you. Walking." I turned my head away.

He wound his window down further and the car crawled along. "I'll take you there."

I stopped. "What, to walking?" I shook my head.

"I'll take you anywhere."

I held my hand up. "No taxi."

"Cheap price." He smiled and nodded vigorously.

"It's okay, we're good." I gave him a thumbs up.

"Where you go? I pick you up afterwards."

I quickened our pace. "No, thank you."

"Darling," Sally said, grabbing my arm, "stop talking to him. You're just encouraging him."

He continued driving alongside us for another five minutes, but I listened to Sally and ignored him. Then he spotted another couple of tourists across the road, did a U-turn, and began stalking them.

"Wow, that was intense," Sally said.

"Wasn't it just?"

Our determination to keep walking paid off. We soon came upon a yacht club, of all things. No doubt in the earlier part of the twentieth century it was a haven for the rich and famous. It cost a quid to enter, and we sat and enjoyed mojitos, the view of the marina, and each other's company. We were the only people in there, and there was no Wi-Fi for Sally, but even that didn't spoil the mood. There was a relaxed vibe about us. My optimism sneaked up little by little the longer we sat and enjoyed the moment, and I felt more determined than ever to win her over.

∽

"Kelly, Kelly, Kelly," Yari said on our return. She mimed eating food.

"What do you think?" Sally asked me. "Shall we eat here tonight?"

"Yeah, why not?" Still feeling relaxed, I was happy to just go with the flow.

Sally held up seven fingers. Yari nodded. Then Sally held her arms aloft and pointed over Yari's head. Yari and I both surveyed the direction she was gesturing to. "I'm trying to tell her *the sea*." Then she placed her knuckles against her eyebrows and waved her fingers.

"Aha. And what's that?" I scratched my head.

"Lobster."

"I think you need to work on your charades skills."

She pointed towards the sea again before pointing upwards and taking Yari's hand. We went upstairs to the terrace.

"Sí. Sí." Yari pointed towards the sea.

Sally leaned forwards and rotated each arm rhythmically.

"Swimming. Sea. Aha. Nice one."

Sally pointed to the sea again and repeated her imitation of a lobster, which could have been mistaken for the *Y* in the "YMCA" dance. Finally, she placed a waggling finger in front of each eye.

"Sí. Sí." Yari giggled and gave us a thumbs up. She seemed to know what Sally meant. I was dubious.

At 7 p.m., as a lightning storm raged, Sally and I were led to an extension of the building, near the back. It was essentially a small, enclosed kitchen with a rickety table. The doorway and the door were different sizes, so the door was held shut with a three-legged chair. I was coming to learn that in Cuba, nothing was thrown away or wasted. It all had a place, even if it offended my sense of order and aesthetics. After serving us more delicious tomato soup, Yari brought out plates of prawns.

I glanced at Sally, and we burst into laughter. Looking confused, Yari imitated Sally's earlier actions and pointed to the plate. I nodded. Close enough. As Yari went to leave, I ushered her towards me. "Yari, do you like Fidel?" My thirst for knowledge about Cuba was aided by alcohol and my good mood.

Her smile slipped.

"Fidel?" I repeated.

Yari glanced from side to side then shuffled from one foot to another, peering down. She held up her thumb. Then she said something in Spanish, tipped her thumb down and spat on the ground. I recoiled slightly, even though the spit had come nowhere near me. The action was shocking. She'd spat in her own kitchen.

"Do you like Cuba?" I asked while gesturing as if to take in the whole country.

She cleared her throat, coughed, nodded, said "Cuba," added something in Spanish, and then held her thumb downwards.

I nodded. This was about as close as I'd got since the taxi driver to having a conversation with a local about Cuba.

By the time we'd finished our meal, the rain had stopped, so we went up to the rooftop terrace and hung over the side drinking Cristal, the local Cuban beer. In the distance, I heard a rumbling noise and voices whooping and hollering. The commotion got louder, and a speck of something turned into a pair of horse-drawn carts.

Outside our accommodation, the carts drew to a halt and lined up. Each one held several occupants drinking from rum bottles. Rum was cheaper than water here. For tourists it was less than two quid; no doubt it was even less for locals. Suddenly the drivers shouted, geed up their horses, and off they went. Laughter filled the post-storm calm of the evening. Seemed we were witnessing the Cuban equivalent of a Roman chariot race.

I stared at Sally, who was caught up in the gladiatorial events below. "Hey, beautiful."

She smiled and looked at me. "I love you, Kevin. You know that don't you?"

I wished I had the confidence to say, *Actually, sometimes I don't know if you truly love me.* "Yeah, I know. And I love you too."

Her smile broadened. "Let's go to bed."

She didn't have to ask me twice.

12

BELLY FLIPS AND SOMERSAULTS

I left Cienfuegos with a full heart. There had been no belly problems the previous night, and my connection with Sally felt stronger than ever. Life was good. Despite Cienfuegos's poverty and lack of things to do, Sally and I had fallen in love with it—and even more with each other, too.

At Casa Yari, Sally had left behind some toiletries, including soap, toothpaste, toothbrushes, and shampoo. I'd read in an online article, that Cubans often had shortages of necessities such as these, so this was our way of showing our appreciation. Yari had been good to us, and Sally felt doing this would be more meaningful than leaving money as a tip.

I'd made little progress on my quest to learn what the locals thought of Cuba, but at least Sally and I were growing closer. We'd had a little adventure so far, but not the Marrakesh kind. Not one that pumped adrenaline through me at an alarming rate. Despite some minor hiccups, everything had gone to plan. I liked that. I loved it, in fact. Me making plans; them happening. Perhaps Marrakesh had been an aberration.

Much wiser than we had been when we arrived, we walked to the bus station (no taxi necessary, thank you!), and I immediately got in the right queue. Unfortunately, that was as far as my good luck extended. I was told that the coach was full up and that I should reserve two seats on a later bus and come back to pay in an hour. The bureaucracy here, and the fact that each place did things differently, drove me crazy. I hated the officiousness and not knowing what was happening. I imagined using an enormous axe to break a big hole in the office door while shouting, "Here's Kevin, and I want to buy my bus tickets!" Of course, I didn't. I went for stoic, as a good Brit.

Before heading to yet another queue, I went to find a toilet to relieve my bladder. My entrance was blocked by a little old lady with a broom, who stretched out a gnarly hand, demanding money. I gave her a dollar, and she stood aside and handed me two sheets of ultra-thin paper. I spied through them and saw the woman. This proved to be the least of my concerns. The stench in the restroom was on par with that which Sally and I had encountered on the promenade the previous day. Worse than our bathroom the night of my belly issues. It was that bad.

I gagged then breathed through my mouth and entered a stall, where I proceeded to dry-heave at the sight before me. The next stall was only marginally better. After doing my business as quickly as possible, I went to flush but found the toilet didn't work, which explained the little brown parcels in the bowl. I tried to wash my hands, but the taps ran empty. I'd officially paid a dollar for two see-through toilet sheets. This won the award for the worst toilet in Cuba.

While Sally played with her phone, I joined the queue early for the next bus, got to the front, paid my money, and was told we had seats on the coach that earlier was full. Elated at my good fortune, I asked, "Do I need to check-in?"

"No."

"Do I need to check our bags in?"

"No."

I grabbed Sally, and we headed jubilantly to the bus. Our progress was halted by an enthusiastic young boy, who demanded we check our bags in—and he wanted money to do it too. Screaming in frustration internally, I obliged handing over a couple of dollars. Afterwards, I stood guard outside the bus, waiting for our bags to be loaded. I waited and waited. No one explained the inexplicable delay.

"Hiya, pal, where you off to?"

A Manchester accent? I spun around. A ginger-haired man about my height stood before me. "Trinidad. You?"

"Same." His head wobbled, and he leaned in conspiratorially. "What do you think of Cuba?"

"Yeah, great, love it so far, except the bus stations and the bureaucracy. They're crap."

"Yeah, I know what you mean. I hate the place. Booked a month and ready to go home now. Nothing to do and the nightlife is shite. The local women are like fridges too. Can't get near them." It had taken him all but six seconds to say *shite*, and he elongated the end of the word in a typical Mancunian way. His negativity grated on me. My mind could provide that aplenty.

Though I had no desire to chat with this bloke, I asked politely, "How long are you in Trinidad for?"

"Not sure, probably a day or so. I'm going to book a flight back." He fidgeted, seemingly unable to stand still for a second.

I dreaded getting into a full-blown conversation with him. His green eyes were intense, and something about him set off an alarm in my head. His gaze darted and stopped on two blonde women behind me. He shoved me out of the way and bustled past.

"Hiya, girls. How's it going? Do you like fish, chips, and mushy peas? Love 'em, I do!"

Not the best chat-up line I'd ever heard, though I didn't

stick around to find out if it worked—finally, our bags were loaded.

After a mercifully uneventful journey, Sally and I stepped off the coach in Trinidad to be besieged by locals holding up signs for their lodgings and stocky men shouting, "TAXI! TAXI!"

My anxiety levels increased exponentially by the second. Nobody was holding up a sign with our names on it. Once again, we'd have to make our own way to our casa particular.

Sally poked me in the ribs. "Darling, what's happening? Where's our transport?"

I scanned around. "Not sure . . . I err . . . follow me." I plodded through the throng. Carrying both backpacks, one on my back, the other on my front, I gripped Sally's hand and led her out of the melee, seeking space and air, but as we moved, so did the crowd surrounding us. Feeling like a victim in a zombie-apocalypse movie, swarmed by ravenous undead, I spotted a gap ahead and cantered as fast as I could under the weight of two backpacks, dragging Sally along with me.

Suddenly, our escape route was blocked by a young local with jet-black hair and the biggest calf muscles I'd ever witnessed up close and personal. "Taxi?"

"Sí. Sí. Yes, please. Thank you." The first one to ask politely; that and the fact that he blocked my path, led me to choose him.

He pointed at the backpacks, which I unfurled from my body. He grabbed one in each hand and beckoned us to follow him out of the chaos. There had to be an unwritten rule amongst taxi drivers because as soon as he claimed us, the swarm dissipated, and we had space to breathe and walk.

A row of yellow taxis lay ahead. We walked past them to a

cycle with a two-seater cart attached. The driver held his hand aloft in the vehicle's direction.

Sally glared at me. "You're joking."

I wished I were. I gaped in disbelief and turned to the driver. "This is our taxi?"

"Yes."

The cycle was elongated and adorned with a blue canopy and a Cuban flag. Our driver placed our backpacks on a shelf underneath the cushioned wooden seat and beckoned us to sit.

Sally folded her arms.

"This is fun, hey?" I said hopefully.

"I don't think so, Kevin."

I climbed aboard and held out my hand to her. "These seats are comfy," I said. "Much better than that horse and cart in Cienfuegos."

"Whatever." She twisted her body away from mine.

The driver turned and addressed me. "You stay?"

I handed him the piece of paper with the address of our casa particular on it and hoped and prayed that our ride would be as short as it had been in Cienfuegos. He began pedalling, and his pert bottom shuffled from side to side.

"Hm, not all bad," Sally said, licking her lips. "I could get used to this."

I placed my palm on her cheek and turned her face, so she was looking at me. I held two fingers to her eyes and then pointed to my eyes. "Keep your eyes on me," I said, forcing a smile. It wore me down, her constant flirting with other men and my never knowing whether my feelings of being disrespected were proportionate or an overreaction.

The cart jolted as its wheel hit a cobblestone. As we gathered speed, the jerking of the wheels on the uneven ground intensified, and with each jerk, my backside left its seat and came down hard. By the time we got to our residence, a bone-crunching fifteen minutes later, my bottom felt as if it had been whipped by an enthusiastic dominatrix.

As the driver unloaded our bags, I knocked on the door of the bungalow and was greeted by a middle-aged woman in a complete flap about something. She spoke quickly and animatedly, flinging her arms about while showing us into our apartment. The place appeared well looked after, and we had two bedrooms, a living room, and a kitchen all to ourselves. Out back was a luscious garden, and the smell of various plants and flowers tickled my nostrils.

Our host kept trying to explain something to us as we looked around. I just shook my head and shrugged. I was getting very skilled at the movement.

"Drinks?" Sally asked, once our host had left. Her face was inscrutable but suspecting that travel-day Sally might be in my presence, I sensed my best move was to agree.

"Yeah, that would be great," I said and ditched our bags in the bigger of the two rooms. "Let's go then."

After conducting a scouting mission of the city that involved taking in the town square and wandering down the narrow lanes and roads that led off it, we found a bar to our liking. Unsurprisingly, it had a rooftop terrace, and we watched the day shift into dusk. A live band belted out a mix of Cuban music, eighties classics, and the occasional modern pop song. Along the street below us were pastel-coloured homes, which gave the scene a vibrant feel.

"This is the life, hey?" I said, after our umpteenth mojito, stretching back into my chair.

Sally sipped her drink. "Hm. Not too bad."

I reached out to hold Sally's hand, but she wriggled away. I studied her. "You okay?"

"Yeah, it's hot and your palm is sweaty. Can't we just sit here and enjoy the music?" She smiled briefly at me before gazing towards the band, at the other end of the bar.

I studied my hand and gave it a little sniff. "Don't think it's sweaty, darling babe."

She slammed her drink down. "Oh, for goodness sake, leave it, Kevin. You're spoiling the moment."

I frowned. Where had I gone wrong? "Sorry, didn't mean to. You are okay, right?"

"YES, I'm FINE."

Oh dear, I was in deep trouble here. She'd used the dreaded F-word. I peeked at her. There was silence for a moment. Then . . .

"Sometimes, you suffocate me to the point where I don't think I can breathe. You're too needy, always seeking affirmation. I can just do without that. That's all."

Her remark about my being too needy struck a nerve. It was something Dawn had accused me of often. I felt it, my neediness, and it was a part of me I despised. Over the years I'd tried unsuccessfully to suppress it, and it had only become worse. "Oh, sorry, I don't mean to do it. I just love you and want to make sure you're okay."

She flung her arms in the air. "That's okay then? Do you think your behaviour is acceptable? You know your problem, Kevin—it's all about you. How about me sometimes?" She thumped her chest.

I tensed. Hang on a minute here. Who'd paid for this trip? Who'd organised it all? I needed a minute. "I'm going to the toilet. Shall we order another lot of mojitos?"

"Yeah, whatever."

In the restroom, I stared at myself in the cracked mirror and shook my head. What had changed since Cienfuegos? Sally's constant mood changes kept me perpetually off balance and unable to settle in the relationship. But, always the peacemaker, I wondered if perhaps she was right—maybe I needed to chill out and not put pressure on her. It had been going so well, and I'd spoilt it. I slapped myself twice across the cheek and winced. The last one stung a little. "Come on, Kevin. Relax."

When I returned to our table, Sally was missing. I scanned the terrace and spotted her talking to the singer of the band, who appeared to be taking a break. *Must be requesting a song.* I squinted to see her through the combination of the setting sun, many mojitos, and my failing eyesight. The man smiled, and she stroked his bicep. Typical Sally—couldn't help but flirt. Her hand lingered. He leant in and said something to her. Then she slapped him on the arm and shook her head with a look of mock horror on her face.

My tummy did a tiny flip. *Don't you start*, I told myself. *They're just talking. Nothing's happening. No need for jealousy here.* My bowels somersaulted backwards. I hated the physical effect my insecurity had on me. Given the conversation we'd just had, I couldn't let Sally see me being jealous.

I sat down as a waitress collected our many empty glasses. "Two more, por favor. Gracias."

Sally returned to the table with a CD. I smiled at her. She eyed me suspiciously and picked up her glass before looking back towards the band. A sly smile lifted the corner of her mouth.

Several mojitos and four more CDs later, we staggered through the central square. Sally stopped. "What time is it?"

I hiccupped and looked at my watch. "Eleven."

"Shall we go home?"

"Yeah." I winked at her. Or maybe it was a blink. Still hadn't mastered the art.

We took several steps, and then Sally suddenly ground to a halt again. "Actually," she said, slurring the word, "you go home. I'm going to explore."

"Nah, I'll come with you. Keep you safe."

"Not this again, Kevin. You go home. I need some space. You're suffocating me." She walked away from me. I walked after her. "Leave me alone."

I watched, crestfallen, as she disappeared up a side street. Finally, I staggered home, replaying the events in my mind, trying to identify my every misstep and mistake. Back in our room, I eyed the pile of clothes and mess on Sally's side and the neat pile of clothes on my side. For a moment, I saw red. Was I angry about the clothes? Or at her? Or both?

I couldn't stop thinking about the exchange I'd witnessed between the singer and Sally, and her words echoed in my head. *"You go home. I need some space."*

My belly flipped and somersaulted out of control. I knew what I had to do next.

13

RAVE IN THE CAVE

I struggled to walk in a straight line as I made my way up the side street where I'd last spotted Sally. It was lined with homes. No bars, restaurants, nothing. I wandered further from the brightly lit centre and climbed steep, rocky terrain, questioning my judgement all the while. Fear crept up and whispered in my ear, "You'll be relieved of your cash, or worse, your kidneys." A calming voice argued, "Cuba is a safe country."

A young couple overtook me. "Rave in the Cave?" one of them asked in an American accent. I nodded. "Follow us." I had no clue what "Rave in the Cave" was, but it sounded like as good a destination as any to look for Sally.

I gasped and stumbled my way up the slope and, after a few minutes, was startled by the sight of some lit-up ruins of a church. *Crikey.* What the hell was I doing? The couple was in front of me, a little distance ahead, I tried desperately to keep within viewing distance of them, so I knew where to go.

Fifteen minutes of hard stomping uphill later, I gazed at an entrance bright and inviting, cut into a cave, having just lost the couple. Inside, I was greeted by a flight of steps from hell—steep, deep, and slippery. I'd had a fear of stairs ever since my sister pushed me down a set when I was a child. To be fair, it was her revenge for all the horrible things I'd done to her, including tying a rope around my neck and telling my nan my sister tried to strangle me. As I was the favourite, my nan believed me. I got the cuddles, and my sister got the punishment.

As I neared the bottom of the stairs, a tunnel that disappeared into the beyond came into view. Excitement filled me, despite the circumstances. I'd been to plenty of raves, but never one in an actual cave, which this appeared to be. I paid the three-dollar entry fee (which included a drink) and wandered through the narrow walkway, which spat me out into an enormous, cavernous space. The Rave in the Cave in all its glory. There were only hints of illumination, which revealed grey walls rising towards the night sky before splintering at the top to let in atmospheric streaks of moonlight.

I was awestruck and mesmerised. Nature in all its glory always bests the world's most prominent architects. I glanced towards the king of the castle. Cocooned in a booth, the DJ reigned high above the dance floor. On either side of his booth was a video screen streaming images to accompany the music blaring out of the speakers.

He weaved a salsa tune into electronic noise, and the sound reverberated around the cave and bounced in a continuous loop off the walls and onto the swaying, sweaty dance floor. The dancers melded into one—a throbbing mass under the spell of the music.

By some miracle I spied Sally, and the jealousy that had been gnawing at me all evening finally exploded. *Told you so!* *s*creamed a voice in my head. Sally and the singer from the rooftop terrace were engaged in their own private dance party within the pulsating crowd. He expertly spun and threw her around the floor before pulling her in close while gyrating his hips and pelvis.

I launched myself towards them. When I was a few feet

away, he said something into her ear. She pulled away, put a finger to her mouth, and then said loudly enough for me to make out, "I'm not that type of girl, but if I was, yeah, I would with you."

That did it. I tapped the guy on the shoulder. Hard. He spun around, smiled, then turned back to Sally. I pulled him round to face me and leant into his ear. "Hey. Can I cut in?" I shifted my gaze to Sally's shocked face.

She glanced from him to me and back again. "Babe. What are you doing here?"

I smiled wryly. "I'm being adventurous. Didn't want to miss the party."

The singer leant in and whispered something to her, but she pulled back and brushed his mouth away. "Darling," she said, looking at me. "I told you I needed some space. Are you stalking me?"

I felt myself shaking with both nerves and self-righteousness. "No. I told you I was feeling adventurous. How was I supposed to know you were coming here? What's going on here?" I gestured to the singer.

She shrugged but wouldn't meet my gaze. "What do you mean?"

"I mean he was gyrating into your crotch and you were up close and personal. That. So, I'll ask again—what the hell were you two doing?"

She looked around, stared downwards, and then gazed at me. She licked her lips then rubbed them. "Oh, darling, it's salsa dancing. That's how they dance here."

"Is it?" I glanced around. "No one else is."

She pushed me away. "Oh, stop it. You shouldn't have come here, followed me here like this. Do you think I've come here to sleep with him?"

I stared at her incredulously. "Strange thing for you to say unless that is what you had in mind."

She clutched her chest. "I can't breathe. I need to get out

of here." She jostled past us. The singer started following her, but I held out my hand and shook my head once. He stopped in his tracks, peered over my shoulder at her, scanned the dance floor, spotted his next victim, and disappeared into the mass of sweating bodies. Good riddance.

I searched the cave and saw Sally climbing the stairs. I ran after her. At the exit, I welcomed a blast of cooler air and then bumped into a Cuban drag queen surrounded by admiring tourists.

Sally had stopped a few feet away and was leaning against an enormous boulder, her shoulders heaving. I held up her face and noticed the lack of tears. "Thank God you came when you did," she said, gasping. "When I arrived, he was here, and suddenly he was all over me. I tried to stop him. I love you, but I just wanted some space tonight and then this happened. I promise I won't leave your side again. I'm only safe when I'm with you."

My anger weakened, despite my knowing it was justified. There was so much more I wanted to say. I'd just found her in the arms of another man, after all. Then again, I thrived on rescuing Sally. Her occasional vulnerability gave me hope that I could be her knight in shining armour. Then I remembered the way they'd been dancing and felt my heart harden again. "Did you kiss?"

"Why would I kiss him?" She looked at me pleadingly.

I eyed her. "Did you kiss?"

She turned away, scanned the ground, stared up at the sky. Finally, her eyes locked on mine. She hesitated. "He tried to kiss me . . ." She sniffled. "Thank goodness you saved me," she blurted. "I love you." She grabbed hold of me and kissed me. "Let's go home."

Rooted to the spot, I tried to take it all in, my brain in overdrive. Yes, I'd seen them up close and personal, but I hadn't caught them in the act of kissing. Maybe Sally was right. Maybe I had rescued her. After all, she was with me now. *Have I won?* She was coming home with me, so yeah, I'd won. I'd beaten him off, protected my woman. We could go back to how things were before this evening. *Everything will be great again*, I told myself loudly, trying to drown out the nagging doubt.

"Come on," I said, "let's get you home."

She fluttered her eyelashes. "Ooooh promises."

As we passed the still-lit-up central square, Sally staggered a little ahead of me and then shrieked. Hopping around, she waved her arms wildly.

I panicked and raced ahead to where she stood. "Wha . . . What? What's up?"

She stamped her feet on the ground and continued waving her arms.

I examined the ground, where I spotted a massive spider. A tarantula, I reckoned; I couldn't remember whether they could kill you. I certainly wouldn't want to salsa with one.

Indifferent to us, it scuttled off.

Sally grabbed me around my neck and kissed me once more. "My Kevin, to the rescue again."

But the mixed feelings continued haunting me as we finally got into bed. Whenever I "rescued" Sally, I'd often be blinded to other stuff going on between us. And I'd been here before. With Dawn.

14

IS IT ME?

The next morning, I shook off the haunting memories and concentrated on a more pressing matter: hunger. My belly rumbled as I left Sally asleep in bed and headed downstairs to the patio in the back garden for breakfast, where a few metal tables and chairs were set out on smooth stones. The space was resplendent, with brightly coloured flowers and plants growing up the walls. Inhaling the sweet, intoxicating aromas, I felt myself relax. For the moment, I'd just enjoy myself and not engage with all my conflicting emotions.

The server was an elderly man named Mario, who moved like a sloth. The growth of hair in each of his flared nostrils seemed about to break open his nose. But the meal was even more fulsome and filling than Yari's: toast, fried eggs, pancakes, ham, cheese, and copious amounts of juice and coffee. As I ate, Ruth, the host, and I repeated our attempts to communicate and failed yet again. She was still in a flap about something, which was a little concerning.

Once Ruth had left, I leant towards a nearby table, where a middle-aged man and woman sat. "Hi, I'm Kevin. Do you speak any Spanish?"

"Yar," said the woman, before taking a huge bite of her toast.

"Oh, great. Ruth has been in a panic since yesterday, but I can't work out what about. Could you ask her and translate?"

"Yar. Of course."

I smiled. "Your accent—where are you from?"

"Germany," she said, before turning back to her partner.

She was certainly economical with her English words. Perhaps she had only a limited supply and didn't want to use them all up. Ruth returned, and in a UN moment, the German woman spoke to her. I listened and watched as Ruth flung her words and arms around with joyful abandon.

The helpful woman nodded and gestured downwards with her hands, in a futile attempt to slow Ruth down, then turned to me. "Yar. Your apartment has two bedrooms. One for you and one for another couple arriving later today."

Aha. "So, the whole place isn't just for us."

"Nein." She shook her head. "No, I mean."

"So, we can only use one bedroom and its en-suite bathroom, and the rest we share?" I raised my eyebrows.

She held up her finger. "I'll check." She spoke once again to the still-energetic Ruth. After plenty of back and forth and nodding, they stared at me and shook their heads. My paranoia shot through the top of my head and into space.

"Yar. That is correct."

I scratched my head. "What is?"

"You each have a bedroom and share the rest of the apartment."

"I'm sure I booked the whole place on the basis we'd be alone," I said, frowning. I was thinking aloud, but my new translator was off again, and I didn't have the courage or language skills to intervene.

Ruth threw her hands in the air then brought them together in a begging motion.

My translator placed a hand on Ruth's arm, stroked it, and turned to me. "She is very sorry."

Ruth gaped at me and clasped her hands, beseeching me to forgive her.

"Whoa, yeah," I said, holding my thumbs up. "That's fine. I don't have any issues. No problem."

Ruth smiled. "Gracias." Then off she trotted.

Of course, she was happy. She'd mastered that capitalist trick of selling the same thing to two different people.

"Thank you so much," I said to the German woman. We were getting nowhere. "Kevin." I pointed to myself.

"Yar, you said." She pointed to herself. "Greta." Then she pointed to her partner. "And this is Tyrone."

Hearing his name, Tyrone paused in his spreading of strawberry jam on toast and looked up at me. "Hey."

I furrowed my brow. "Oh, you don't sound German?"

He sat back in his chair and gulped coffee. "No, I'm American. I live in Germany now."

"Excellent." I shuffled my chair a little closer. "What's the story with our waiter?"

He studied the house. "You mean Mario? He's Ruth's husband. Fascinating man. Used to be a doctor. Retired now, though."

Happy days! If I exploded from overeating, he could stitch me back together.

"You alone?" Greta asked.

"No, my girlfriend is having a little lie-in. Had a bit of a late night." I made a drunk face and added, "If you know what I mean." A flashback of Sally in the singer's arms invaded my head. I blinked to eject it.

Just then Sally emerged into the patio area and came towards me. "Morning, darling," she said.

"Speak of the devil and she shall appear," I said to my new friends. "Morning, babe. How are you feeling?"

She held out her hand and shook it from side to side.

"That good, hey." I stood and pulled out a chair for Sally, who slumped down. I returned to my seat. "Let me introduce you to Greta and Tyrone," I said, gesturing. Sally nodded at the couple. They nodded back. "Greta has solved the mystery of Ruth's panic," I continued. "We don't have two bedrooms anymore." Sally frowned. "Don't worry, we're fine. Everything's excellent."

She studied my face. "You seem chipper." Then she smiled weakly. "Listen, about last night . . ."

I held up a finger to shush her and accidentally slipped it into her mouth. I quickly snatched it away. "Nothing to say. You're here with me now, so let's forget about last night. It didn't happen."

The conversations with Greta, Ruth and Tyrone had cheered me up, and in my head, the voice telling me to focus on winning over Sally and forgetting last night had gained a small but significant foothold.

Sally stared at me intensely, frowned a little, and then smiled. "You're the best, darling, and nothing happened. I'm here with you now."

"Exactly." I picked up the coffeepot Ruth had left me and poured us each a coffee. Taking a sip, I gazed up at the blue sky. The weather in Trinidad was warmer than it had been in Cienfuegos. On our last day there, the temperature had dipped into the low twenties, Celsius, and I swear dogs shivered in the street.

"Darling, can we find some Wi-Fi today?"

Access to the internet didn't involve Cuban spivs with black boxes trying to sell us "The Internet". No, that would have been easier than what transpired.

Sally sat in a park while across the road, I queued outside the state-owned telecommunications shop that Greta and

Tyrone had told me about. The orderly queue of tourists had formed alongside a queue of locals—an anarchic, seething, and ever-moving mass. A local would get in the queue, shout "Ultimo", disappear, come back and shout "El Ultimo", and join further up the line. Our system seemed polite and boring in comparison.

The shop had a statuesque guard who let people from both lines in and out with no discernible policy or procedure.

There was a tap on my shoulder. I swivelled around, and the guy behind me said, "Excuse me, what's the situation with the Cuban line and 'ultimo'?"

I shrugged, but the woman in front of me chimed in. "Their system for queuing means they find out who joined the queue just before them, keep track of that person, and then join and leave the line at will."

We thanked her, and I watched as an old Cuban guy shouted "Ultimo", left the queue, and sat across the road in the park. I could see the sense and the logic of it, but I was British. We're masters of queuing. I've witnessed near-riots of tutting and shaking of heads if a person pushes in front of a queue. And there's always one brazen individual who'll shout their displeasure: "There's a queue here, you know." But this person is as much a pariah as the queue-jumper.

After an hour under the scorching sun, my nerves were fraying, and my resentment was building. In a moment of panic—exhausted and fearing the repercussions if I returned to Sally empty-handed—I threw myself at the mercy of a German man at the front of the queue. I gave him a bundle of Cuban dollars, probably more than was necessary, and begged him for some Wi-Fi vouchers. This opened the floodgates. Several other tourists besieged him, a few of whom were in tears. He relented, and minutes later the unsmiling guard ushered him into the inner sanctum. He emerged a while later, triumphant, like a spotty teenager who's just lost his virginity. I grabbed the vouchers and returned to Sally, displaying my treasure.

The next challenge was trying to find a Wi-Fi spot. I stared at my phone, watching the signal rise and fall, before settling under a tree, where the signal seemed decent enough. I gestured Sally over then scraped away the silver covering on what looked like gambling scratch cards to reveal our codes, usernames, and passwords to access the Wi-Fi. Around us, Cubans huddled in groups passing phones around and taking turns speaking. Some conducted video chats where everyone tried to squeeze into the shot. Meanwhile, Sally and I ignored each other, heads down, staring at our phones.

I messaged my parents and sons to tell them I was safe and in Trinidad. Then onto important business. Everton, my football team, hadn't lost their last game. Hurrah. I'd also received a message from our accommodation in the Cayman Islands: the hosts had changed their mind, meaning we had nowhere to stay. I cursed and quickly found another available home for rent. My communications completed, I wiggled over to Sally and peered over her shoulder. She was oblivious to my presence. I spied a text to her from an old friend whom she'd not seen in ages asking if she was "still going out with that bloke".

I continued watching as she typed: *NO, thank god. What I ever saw in him I'll never understand.*

My chest tightened. Did she mean me? I quickly dismissed the idea. Couldn't be me. We were still together. She had to be talking about John, the guy she'd been seeing when she and I first started seeing each other. Such is modern romance. Had to be him. No other logical explanation for her saying what she said.

My thoughts shifted. I hadn't realised that she and her old friend were talking again. They'd had a massive falling-out. I never got all the details regarding Sally's many fallings-out with family and friends. All I knew was that it was always the other person's fault. I'd console her in the aftermath, offering a listening ear and a shoulder to cry on. During these times, I'd hope she'd feel that I could rescue her from the pain of life.

As I thought about this now, the nagging doubt that had plagued me the previous evening returned, looming larger than before. I couldn't confront Sally about the text, as I'd been snooping. But I couldn't let it go either. Something didn't feel right, and I needed to put my finger on what was off, one way or another, by the end of the holiday. I owed myself that.

That evening, we headed to a paladar that our guidebook had recommended. It was supposedly the best one in the whole of Trinidad. When we reached it, I turned to Sally. "Are you sure this is the right place?"

The door was closed. No light or noise emanated from the building, and no other people were around.

She pushed me forward. "Yes."

I stepped back and studied the place. "Babe, it doesn't look open."

She waved her hand towards the door. "Try it."

I did, but the door wouldn't budge. The place spooked me. I felt as if I were trying to intrude into someone's home. I scratched my head. "Let me have the book."

Sally rummaged in her bag, pulled out the guidebook, and plonked it in my outstretched hand. I found the page I was looking for and double-checked the address. This was the place.

"Knock on the door."

"You knock on the door," I said, trying to push her forward.

"Oh, for God's sake," she said, digging her heels in.

I sighed, stepped forward, and banged on the door.

"Louder."

"Harrumph." I rapped it louder and then put my ear to the door just as it opened inwards.

I sprang back. "Oh, hi, yeah, erm, restaurant?"

The woman contemplated me, stuck her head forward and glanced up and down the street, then looked back at me. "No food. All gone."

"What?"

"No food. All gone." She stepped back and slammed the door in my face.

The best paladar in Trinidad, closed because it had run out of food. This was a first for me. I imagined the place being featured on television. With a liberal sprinkling of foul language, a celebrity chef would do their nut about running out of food and letting down customers.

"Closed."

Sally placed her hands on her hips. "What now?"

I twiddled my lips. "How about that fun place from last night, where we sat outside?" Not the one with the singer I'd found Sally with. This establishment had an older, less attractive singer.

Sally shook her head. "I remember a couple of places like that."

"Come." I took her hand and tugged gently. "I'll take us."

I smiled as we reached the place, minutes later. "Bound to be a fantastic meal here." As we walked through the restaurant to a courtyard at the back, I realised that the mojitos I'd consumed the previous day might have given me a perspective of the place that was vastly different from my relatively sober one. The paint peeled off the walls, none of the tables or chairs matched, and the tablecloths were stained. Once we were seated, we were less than thrilled to learn that the service was slow, and the dishes were lukewarm.

During our meal, guests kept walking past our table and pointing and staring at a cage about ten feet behind us.

Finally, curiosity got the better of me. I wandered over, peered in, and . . . "Oh my God," I whispered.

I returned to our table shaking my head.

"What's up?" Sally looked concerned.

"You will not believe it. Come here."

She remained seated. "What? Tell me."

I beckoned her. "No, you need to see this for yourself."

Conceding, Sally stood and followed me back to the cage, where her mouth dropped open. She swivelled to me. "You're kidding me. That's a . . ."

"Yes, a crocodile in a cage, right next to where we're eating."

She bent down for a closer look. "Not moving, though. Perhaps it's plastic."

"Excuse me," I said, flagging down a passing waiter. "Is this real?" I pointed at the cage.

"Sí." He frowned at me as if he were talking to the village idiot.

My complete shock gave way to sadness. Poor crocodile stuck in a cage barely bigger than itself. We finished our meal and left immediately. Just when I thought I was getting to grips with the country, the best paladar runs out of food and we end up in a restaurant with a live crocodile. We headed to a nearby bar for a debrief, which involved drinking copious quantities of mojitos.

At one point, Sally went to the toilet. When she hadn't returned fifteen minutes later, I started worrying. It didn't take me long to find her at the back of the establishment chatting to a waiter. I waved at her and approached. "I was concerned," I said.

She shook her head and followed me back to our table. "I was trying to find the best beach around here. There's one not too far away, a taxi ride from here."

"What, now?"

"No, tomorrow." She sighed exasperatedly then slammed

her purse on the table. "Why did you follow me? Monitoring me? Making sure I'm not talking to men again?"

I slumped into my chair. "You'd been gone ages. I wanted to make sure you were okay. Sorry for caring and all that." Half the truth. After last night's events, my paranoia about her flirting was heightened.

"Oh, don't give me that. Let's go. I don't want to be here anymore. I want to go home." She stalked out, and I hurried after her.

"That's not the way home," I said, catching her arm just before she turned a corner. I bent over and breathed heavily after the exertion of catching her up.

Sally surveyed the surroundings. "How do you know?"

"Because I have the map here and this is the way home." I waved the guidebook then straightened and began walking along the street I was certain took us back.

Sally stayed a couple of steps behind me. "You've always got to be right, haven't you?"

I stopped and turned towards her with a sigh. I'd made a mental note of the route, as usual, knowing that there'd be an argument if I couldn't find our way home. Now we were arguing because I did know the way. I couldn't win, whatever I did. "No, I haven't. It's just that I know the way back. Come with me." I held out my hand.

She folded her arms. "No. I'll go where and how I want to."

I tilted my head and peered along the ground at the non-existent spiders and creepy crawlies, hoping to distract her. "I'm worried about tarantulas after last night."

Sally lifted a leg and hopped on the spot. "What? Where? Did you spot one?"

"No, but just in case." I ushered her to me. "Come on."

She walked alongside me, but two metres to my left. When we got back to our place, I tried to hide my triumph. Badly.

She twisted her mouth. "My way would have got us back too. You're not always right."

I pulled the keys out of my pocket and opened the door. "Come on, let's go to bed."

She didn't budge. "No. I'll come in when I want."

Five minutes after me, Sally climbed into bed and faced the wall. Exhausted, all I wanted was to sleep. Instead, I lay on my back and stared at the ceiling as my racing mind contemplated why exactly we were fighting again and what I could do to end the cycle.

15

LIGHTNING CAN STRIKE TWICE

"We sit here," Greta said, pointing at the two empty chairs at my and Sally's table on the back patio. It was more of an instruction than a question.

"Yes, please do." I moved my chair a little closer to Sally's. Her eyes shot daggers at me. We'd barely exchanged any words since getting up. Given the frosty atmosphere between us, I was surprised Greta and Tyrone wanted to sit with us for breakfast.

Tyrone leant in and whispered in my ear, "I didn't want to come to Cuba. I wanted to build a biological lab in our basement."

Lovely to meet you too, mate. What the actual . . .? I smiled weakly and turned to Greta. "Thanks for the recommendation on the Wi-Fi vouchers—worked a treat."

Greta nodded.

"You realise they're spying on you, don't you?" Tyrone's eyes darted from side to side.

I choked a little on my toast. "Sorry. What? Who?"

He leant in further. "The government." Then he sat back.

I gulped some coffee. "The Cubans?" I'd expected they

would be. I mean, communist, totalitarian state. Of course, they were spying on us.

He shook his head and let out a weary laugh. "No, THE government."

"Oh, you mean the American one." I winked at him, hoping it didn't come across flirtatiously, as my inability to wink properly was still an issue for me.

"No. THE World Government. UN and all those guys."

Now, I prided myself on my knowledge of current affairs. I'd even visited the UN's headquarters in Geneva with my sons, who'd ended up having a massive fight about the path to world peace, or the best player on the video game *FIFA*. One or the other. I believed the organisation had its heart in the right place but was ineffectual, given the various vetoes that the bigger countries had. But nowhere had I read it was THE World Government.

"Oh, okay." I spread jam on a piece of toast and tried to hide my scepticism. "Didn't realise that."

He pointed at the plate of toast and raised an eyebrow. I gestured for him to take a piece. "Yeah," he said, carefully buttering a slice. "They're trying to construct a new world order, a one-world government."

"How interesting." I kicked Sally under the table. She glared at me then returned to her conversation with Greta.

"Hi, can I sit down?"

I peeked up to see a pretty young woman standing at the table. "Yeah, sure. Hey, I'm Kevin."

"Jenny," the woman said, shaking my proffered hand. She had blonde hair, piercing blue eyes, and an accent. And of course, I was hopeless at identifying it.

Sally gave me a look that a hydra would have been proud of then inched her chair right next to mine. "Hiya," she said, looking up at Jenny. "We've not been introduced. I'm Sally, Kevin's girlfriend." She grabbed hold of my hand and smiled at me. "So, my lovely boyfriend, Greta has been telling me all about a beautiful beach nearby."

Only moments ago, Sally had been ignoring me. Then Jenny appears and suddenly, I'm Sally's and Sally's alone. It had happened a couple of times before. Usually, I revelled in her attentions. This time, I wondered why she couldn't just give me this kind of attention even when she didn't feel threatened. I took another bite of my toast and savoured the homemade strawberry jam. "Let's leave the beach to another day. It's cloudier today. I say explore."

"Ooooh, look at you, being all masterful." She forced out a laugh.

"That's decided then."

As breakfast continued, I did my best to drown out Tyrone's ravings but caught the occasional word: "Infection . . . Cure . . . Ebola . . . What do you think?"

You're madder than a box of frogs is what I think. Either he was telling me he'd invented Ebola or had found a cure for it. Or both.

"Wow, amazing." *It would be more amazing if I could escape this conversation.* I shifted my mug of coffee closer to my body. I didn't want him slipping a microbe or billion into my digestive system. This was the closest I'd ever come to a dangerous scientist, who could accidentally kill lots of people. I grabbed the last piece of toast.

"Let me know when you guys end up going to the beach," Jenny said. "We can share a taxi."

"Yeah," I said, "that would be amazing. Meet us here for breakfast tomorrow and we'll take it from there." I couldn't deny that she was attractive, and Sally's lack of interest in me often left me desperate for it elsewhere. That said, while it gave me a warm glow to receive attention from other women, I'd never act on it. I knew Jenny was not the answer to my problems.

Sally poked me in the ribs. "Come on, boyfriend, let's get

ready and start exploring this town." She stood and pulled me up with her. Aha, a brilliant escape—evoke petty jealousy in Sally, who would then prise me away from Billy the Bullshitter.

Once we were back in our apartment, Sally's smile vanished, and she got right in my space, one hand on her dropped hip, the other gesticulating wildly. "What the hell did you invite her for?"

I backed away and hit the wall. "Eh? She's on her own. Seemed a kind thing to do."

"Yeah?" she said, poking my chest. "Would you have done the same if it were a bloke?"

"Yes," I said and meant it.

"Liar," she spat.

"No, I would . . ." The raised pitch of my voice made me grimace.

"Bit defensive there, Kevin. We both know the truth." Her eyes narrowed, and she stepped back. "Get ready. We're going out."

I nodded meekly. Yeah, well, I wouldn't be salsa dancing up close and personal with Jenny, that was for sure.

We wandered Trinidad's back streets in silence. Sally seemed ready to explode again, so I did my best to focus on my surroundings and not set her off. Despite the heat and 1950s-style exhaust fumes, the city was, overall, a breath of fresh air: it had soul. Good energy, food (unless the restaurant had run out), and drink, of course. The days were quiet, but at night the city came alive with music, singing, and dancing, and the vibe was exuberant.

It felt different from Cienfuegos and Havana. It had its own identity. It was a city that felt like a large village stuck in a time warp, with its colonial-style mansions. Everything was perfectly preserved. I also noticed how rife with tourists it was, but a more distinctive kind of tourist—people who were intrigued and keen to explore on their own, rather than in large, guided tours.

I caught a whiff of sickly-sweet sugar cane as we came upon a small market. Then, just as we had been when we first arrived in Trinidad, at the coach station, we were besieged by local touts. "Man buys! Lady buys!" they shouted, as they thrust their wares—primarily overpriced, poorly made wooden objects—into our vision.

I'd read in my guidebook that Trinidad's growing tourism had led to a subculture of hustling and hassling so strong that you might wonder whether your name was actually "Man Buy". Restaurant touts, tour touts, and even casa touts would stand outside competitors' businesses and tell you they were full when they weren't. I never felt threatened, as I had in Marrakesh, but the overselling meant that instead of loving Trinidad, I liked it.

"NO, thank you," I repeated firmly.

"Oh, darling, look at this," Sally said, pointing to something. Seemed she'd forgotten she was meant to be ignoring me. "A small wooden chess set with plastic pieces. Harry would love this."

I checked it out; it looked cheap. "I could buy him a proper one."

"Not one made in Cuba, though." She picked it up. "How much?" she asked the vendor.

I walked away to let her barter. When she rejoined me, we stopped at a restaurant in a courtyard. A female singer was serenading the diners, all tourists. I felt the frost between Sally and me beginning to thaw. She reached over and momentarily held my hand. Then she smiled at me before returning her gaze to the singer.

I flagged down a waitress. "Dos Cristal, por favor."

She bowed. "Please, señor, try Hatuey."

"Beer?"

"Si, señor."

Hatuey was a new one on me. So far, I'd found two major beer brands in Cuba: Cristal and Bucanero. Cristal was a mid-strength lager and decent tasting. Bucanero, on the other hand, would knock your socks off as a result of both its taste and alcohol content. The waitress returned with two bottles that featured a Native American on the logo. This logo was yet another mystery in this country. I took one swig and spat the overly sweet liquid back into the bottle.

"Eurgh, disgusting." I wished I had a supply of mints on hand.

"What's up?" Sally asked.

I shook the bottle in the air then placed it on the table. "Foul. Don't allow a drop to pass your lips."

Ever defiant, Sally picked up her bottle, took a swig, screwed up her face, and swallowed like a pro.

"You could have spat it out, babe."

"You know me, darling—always swallow, never spit."

Not true. Not for a long time, anyway. I laughed though, and the tension eased more. I ordered two Cristal, "Stick with what you know" being my new motto. Why had the server recommended Hatuey? Commission? Possibly. Trying to get rid of them due to their awful taste? More likely.

Suddenly, in the middle of a song, the singer stopped and scanned the audience, clearly seeking a partner. Noticing this, Sally jumped up and pointed at me. I groaned internally. I'd done plenty of public speaking in my time, both as a former trade unionist and in my current job at the housing association, but I was uncomfortable with anything that involved getting up to do something unknown in front of people who'd all stare and laugh.

I begrudgingly stood, and the singer pulled me into her arms to dance with me. We swayed awkwardly from side to side. Noticing Sally recording the proceedings and laughing, I shot her a glare. As I did, I lost my footing and fell to the side, pulling the singer down on top of me. In a moment of panic, I let out a screech. I'm claustrophobic, and she had a fair bit of weight on her. I wriggled and wriggled until I'd extracted myself then took deep breaths and waited for my panic to subside.

When I stood, I saw the singer sitting on a chair being fanned by a waiter. I avoided his gaze, hung my head, and returned to our table, my face flushed not from exertion or heat but embarrassment.

Sally was laughing uproariously. "That's going on my Facebook page." A giggle got caught in her throat, and she coughed before continuing. "I can't believe you tried to shag her in front of everybody."

"Actually, she mounted me."

"Oh, dear." She took a tissue out of her bag to mop up her tears. "In your dreams."

I gazed up at the sky, still trying to compose myself. Then something Sally had said registered. I jerked my head towards her. "I thought you'd come off."

"What?" Sally looked puzzled.

"Facebook." I studied her face.

"Oh, yeah . . ." She looked away and took a sip of beer. "I did, but back on now."

"Oh, have you accepted my friend request?" I said.

"Can't remember, darling. I'll probably come off again soon, so not worth it. Come on, let's finish up and explore some more." She swigged back the last of her beer.

I ripped off the label on my bottle. A Facebook incident had triggered an argument between Dawn and me that ultimately ended the relationship. I hated that Sally hadn't told me she was back on the site and was refusing to accept my friend request. Made me wonder what she was hiding. "Do you post about us?"

"Of course." She stood. "You're my boyfriend."

I could have sworn that the last time I'd tried, I couldn't find her on Facebook, but that had been a while ago.

"Come on, let's go." She ushered me to follow her.

As we headed away from the restaurant along a side street, we came upon a group of old Cuban men playing dominoes. Suddenly, one of them flipped up the table. Another stood, and they got in each other's faces. Fellow players and spectators tried to separate them, but they were both furious and determined to have it out with each other. I thought I heard one of them yell *"Bastardas!"* Fascinated by this microcosm of life in another country, I wanted to watch to see if they would kick off, but Sally tugged me away from the scene. Shame. My money was on Baldy. He had a mean face and, I reckoned, a temperament to match. Sturdy and barrel-chested, he would have knocked the hell out of the other guy, all skin and bones.

As the afternoon faded, we found ourselves in the town square watching a dance performance that depicted the history of Cuba. It was exceptionally entertaining: the dancers; the flashy, clashing costumes; the whirling, stomping, singing—well, not singing, more shouting. There were representations of slaves, pirates, and Fidel and the revolution, and a load of blokes beating bongos senseless. For each scene, there was a costume change. Mesmerised, I could have watched for hours. It was over too soon.

I turned to Sally. "Wow, that was amazing and intense."

She smiled. "Not the best singing I've ever heard, but the performance carries you along." She grabbed the arm of a passer-by. "Are there any good places nearby to listen to music?"

"Sí, Casa de la Música." He gave us directions.

The place turned out to be an outdoor venue packed with tourists. I immediately knew it wasn't my scene. Standing there in a pair of faded jean shorts and an un-ironed short-sleeved shirt, I inspected the men, all tourists, who wore smart trousers and pressed shirts. I'd much rather observe old Cuban men arguing over dominoes than spend time in a place where stylish tourists were sipping mojitos and having their every whim and need tended to, not attempting to engage with the locals. Plus, the music was decidedly not Cuban. It reminded me of a five-star resort Sally and I had visited in Marrakesh.

I'd thought that's what I wanted in a vacation. Not anymore. I wanted something else. Something less . . . mainstream. Something more me. Whatever I was. I was still searching for that. The proverbial missing piece. That thing that would fix me and maybe Sally and me too. I was suddenly reminded that I needed to find out the truth before the end of this holiday. At that moment, sadness and grief washed over me. And, despite Sally's presence, loneliness too.

In a sudden burst of spontaneity, wanting to "live a little", I persuaded her to hitch a ride back to our casa in a cycle taxi.

The next morning, I awoke with a tender bottom. What had seemed a fantastic idea quickly transformed into a near disaster. I'd forgotten that the streets were cobbled and riddled with potholes, including one nearly the size of the Grand Canyon—a dream for accident claim lines. Not that they existed in Cuba, which only endeared the country to me more. An aspect of Western culture I disliked was the ease with which one could reach out to a solicitor to solve a problem. Maybe a carry-over from my divorce? Or a case of "whatever happened to talking and resolving differences"? At any rate, I'd got off the cycle doing my best John Wayne impression.

The pain was excruciating, but not worse than Sally's mood when we got back. I'd attempted to ease the tension with a joke about how we now understood what it was like to be buggered by a large mammal. She didn't laugh. I swear I heard her mutter "twat" under her breath.

At breakfast, I once again found myself sat next to Tyrone. I zoned in and out of the conversation.

"New world order . . . Freedom . . . Experiments . . . UN . . . Totalitarians . . . Cuba."

"Hmm . . . Yes . . . Wow . . . Interesting . . . So glad you told me that."

This version of Walter White—who instead of crystal meth wanted to cook up the biological equivalent of the four horsemen of the apocalypse—wouldn't shut up, and I worried that simply talking to him could lead to my arrest and interrogation. Would I be considered an accessory?

I turned to Sally and tried to change the subject. "Sun's out, gun's out." I kissed my biceps and cricked my neck. "Are we going to the beach today?"

"'Sun's out, gun's out'? Where the hell did you learn that?"

I shrugged. "Probably one of my sons."

"Please don't use phrases like that," she said, buttering her toast. "So, unbecoming."

I felt as if I were a child being told off for being naughty. My resentment building, I turned to the table next to ours. "You still coming, Jenny?"

"Yeah, if it's okay with you both." She stared at Sally.

"Course it is, isn't it, Sal?" I nudged her.

Sally widened her mouth into a shape that resembled a smile. "Yes, darling, we'd love to have you along. Must be lonely on your own. How come you're solo?"

Jenny stared into space momentarily. "Booked it with my boyfriend. We split up before the holiday and I thought, what the hell, I'll still go."

I nodded. Brave woman. I wouldn't have come on my own if Sally and I had broken up. "That's very adventurous of you."

After breakfast, we found a jeep to taxi us to the beach, where the three of us spent the morning sunbathing. Sally interacted with Jenny, all polite and adult. But I saw in the way she forced her smiles that it was a show. Around noon, I found myself at the edge of the water with Jenny. Sally had spread-eagled herself on a towel several feet away, creating the maximum surface area for attracting the sun.

We dipped our toes in the water. "People have been kind to me," Jenny said. "Better for me to be at the beach with you two. Otherwise, I'd attract unwanted attention from the local men. They assume if I'm on my own, I'm fair game."

I shook my head. "I don't understand how that must feel for you as a single woman, travelling alone. I've never travelled on my own—too many fears and anxieties." I stared down as we moved a little further into the water, wishing I could be as brave as Jenny but knowing that would likely never happen.

"To be honest, other than that, it's been great for me," she continued. "Made me realise I do like my own company, and that means I won't fall into the trap of getting into another bad relationship just so I have someone to travel or do stuff with."

Sadness gripped me. I was uncomfortable in my own company, unable to get by unless I was in a relationship. In essence, I was trapped, to use Jenny's word, in what was increasingly feeling like another bad relationship.

"DARLING." I turned round to see Sally stood up, hands on her hips. "Can you come here, please? Shouted to you three times already."

Jenny twisted around then looked at me. "Is she okay? Seems kind of angry."

I sighed. "Her natural state of being. I'll see what's up." I trudged through the sand to Sally, who manoeuvred herself so I wouldn't be able to see Jenny, still at the water's edge. "What the hell are you doing?"

"What do you mean?" I stammered.

"We're the couple, yet you've spent all day chatting to her." She gestured behind her with her thumb.

I held up my hands in mock surrender. "I thought you wanted to lounge in the sun."

"I do, but I don't want you talking to her."

My hands flopped to my sides. "Why?"

"Because she's bad news. She's flirting with you and you're encouraging her. I can see you're flattered by her attention."

"That's not how it is." I stepped towards her. "Do you want me to stay here and talk to you?"

She stepped back. "No, I just want you to lie here." She pointed to my towel, unfurled next to hers.

I stared at the towel and back at Sally. "What, no talking?"

"No." She shooed me away.

"You're being unreasonable. I don't want to lie in the sun. I'm going in the water. You coming?" I turned and began walking back to the water. Wow, that had felt good, sticking up for myself. I needed to do that more often.

"No, thank you, don't want to interrupt your private party with Jenny." Each syllable sizzled with sarcasm. I kept walking. "Darling." A more conciliatory tone. "Could you put some cream on my back?"

I traipsed back. "Yes, dear." I was frustrated by her attitude and wondering where the jealousy came from, my reluctance to be in her presence was very obvious.

Once I'd rubbed the cream in, I headed back to the sea's edge.

"Is she okay?" Jenny asked.

"Not sure," I said, staring out at the water. I was never sure anymore.

Jenny cleared her throat, and out of the corner of my eye, I saw her glance at me. "Part of the reason my last relationship ended was that my boyfriend was controlling and jealous. At first, I thought it was because he loved and adored me, but it got worse the longer we were together."

I faced her. "What happened?"

She met my gaze. "Funny that—turned out he cheated on me."

Tightness gripped my stomach momentarily. "Huh, so after all that, all his jealousy, he was the one cheating on you." I shook my head. I could relate. "I was in a relationship where the same thing happened. Kind of more complicated, but similar."

"What about this one? No doubts, no suspicions?"

I laughed without humour. She was picking up on what I hadn't wanted to admit. "Plenty of them, but no proof—not enough, at least. And I wonder if perhaps I'm viewing Sally through the lens of being hurt before."

"Lightning can strike in the same spot twice." She gazed at me sympathetically.

"I hope not," I said with a sigh. "I'd be devastated."

"No harm in investigating more."

"You might be right on that." Turning, I spotted Sally chatting to a local man. She glanced over at me and then shooed him away.

Frowning, I returned to my towel to check on Sally. When I was within a couple of feet of her, Sally gazed up at me. "Do you think she's beautiful?"

"Jenny? Yeah, why?"

"Nice figure?"

I knelt. "She clearly looks after herself."

"What, unlike me?"

I reached out, but she pulled away. "Babe, you're gorgeous, and I love your body." I lunged forward and grappled her, but she wriggled away, her face fierce. Yikes. I'd forgotten the first rule of our relationship: never, ever tell Sally that another woman is good-looking.

"I knew you fancied her. Can't believe you're trying to cheat on me with her of all people." She stood and loomed over me.

I quickly got to my feet. "I'm not. And it's not as if you

don't find other guys good-looking. You fancy that bloke who plays Luther."

"It's not the same thing." She turned away from me.

"What about that guy from the cave the other night?" I said evenly.

Her head twisted around, reminding me of a possessed person in a horror movie. I stepped back. "DON'T change the subject. I've caught you out." She fully twirled around and thrust a finger in my face. "I want to go back."

"Okay, shall I tell her?" I turned towards Jenny, who was oblivious to the raging argument her presence had sparked.

Sally bent down and yanked up her towel. "No, I want to go back without her."

I took a few steps towards the water. "At least let me tell her."

"NO."

Not wanting this to be the hill that I died on, I gathered my belongings and took one last look at Jenny, who waved. I discreetly waved back.

My mood improved marginally when I negotiated a seven-dollar taxi ride back—one dollar less than our journey to the beach had been. As we walked to the "taxi", I realised why. The car resembled a decrepit Reliant Robin. I'd forgotten when booking a cab in Cuba: ask to inspect the car first. God only knew if we'd make it back to our place in one piece.

I got in the front, Sally in the back, and the driver produced a part from his pocket. Oh, my lord, a screw-in handle for the choke. With great concentration and precision, he achieved the exact amount of choke and gas necessary, and after ten long minutes, we set off.

The worst was yet to come. The driver couldn't bring the vehicle to a complete stop, as it would stall, and as we approached a railway junction, a train trundled along the track. There was no way on earth we'd make it across in time. In my head, we crashed into the train and died. I closed my eyes then opened them. Terror consumed my body. As we got nearer, he slowed down and did not a U-turn but an O-turn. Two of them, in fact, and by the end of our second rotation, the train had passed.

Thank goodness for the bottle of rum waiting for us in our casa—a thank-you from Ruth for the bedroom situation. Such a sweet gesture.

Sally and I hadn't exchanged a word since the beach, and the silence continued over dinner, the only sound the clacking of our cutlery on our plates. I played with my food, not hungry. Normally I would have apologised by now. I hated this kind of tension. But I couldn't bring myself to smooth things over just yet. What did I have to apologise for, after all?

16

HOMELESS IN VARADERO

My heart was heavy as we prepared to leave Trinidad. I wanted to stay. The place had character, and something about it had spoken to me, had flicked a switch in me. Plus, I felt myself hurtling towards a denouement with Sally. I was losing her, which was the last thing I wanted.

But I also couldn't ignore the growing feeling that our status quo just wasn't working anymore.

We would be travelling to Varadero via taxi. And not just any old taxi but a *Colectivo*, a shared cab that operated on a standard route. The taxi might be a normal car, or it might be a classic one. I wondered whether classic might not equate to cool—just ancient and on the verge of breaking down?

I'd booked the service so we could get to the resort quicker than by coach and take advantage of the all-inclusive drinks. The booking had been a concession to Sally, who wanted a nice place to stay from Christmas Eve through to the day after Boxing Day.

Our taxi driver turned up, but then a man who looked just like him turned up and got in the driver's seat. Our original driver moved to the passenger seat. We travelled for a few minutes, the driver got out, and then another man got into the driver's seat. Confused? Because I was! We drove for a few more minutes then stopped and waited for ages outside a casa. Finally, a lovely couple from Canada joined. When the new couple got in the car, Sally made me swap seats with her, as she said it wasn't appropriate for me to sit next to another woman squashed up in a taxi. The first words we'd exchanged since the beach.

The most recent driver buggered off, the original driver jumped into the driver's seat, and we finally made our way to Varadero with no more stops. I'd already learned that many Cuban taxi drivers used their horn for two major reasons: to inform other drivers of their sincerely held belief that their driving skills were better and to alert young ladies that they were horny. But my education on Cuban taxi drivers wasn't over. At one point, the driver, having finished a can of pop, tossed it out the window as if this were normal behaviour. After that, I took note of the rubbish-filled ditches. I'd imagined Cubans would be fastidious about keeping their country clean, but when I asked the driver about this, he told me that the government employed people to pick up rubbish. Therefore, by littering, he was performing a civic duty.

I tried to see it from his point of view but could only conclude the man was a litter lout. Plus, the mess alongside the roads negated the argument that someone was employed to pick it up. A blessing and a curse of mine, was always wanting to see an issue from somebody else's perspective. I wondered if this tendency was in play with Sally, given how I always made excuses for her. *She's a grown woman,* I thought. *She can speak for herself.* I had to concentrate on my views, whatever they truly were.

I still had to confront her about the Facebook issue, the text messages I'd seen, the incident with the singer—a growing list pointing to her untrustworthiness. "Do it after the holiday" had become my mantra. Or maybe there was another way. One I'd used in the past. The nuclear option.

In the meantime, I made a mental note to not make excuses for her anymore. I also had to make sure I took the high and moral ground so as not to give her any reason to accuse me of being untrustworthy. I couldn't fight dirty. I didn't think that would be too hard. It was unlike me to deliberately set out to hurt another person.

I mmediately after dumping our bags in our hotel room in Varadero, Sally and I set off in search of a bar, keen to take advantage of the all-inclusive package. The hotel appeared fairly modern; the lobby was busy and spacious, and the complex stretched way beyond the confines of the main building.

Once seated at an outdoor bar, with our plastic cups, which we'd been instructed to keep hold of, I inspected the other guests. Many of them had brought their own glasses, larger than our regulation ones. We'd missed a trick here. And I couldn't help but notice that most of them appeared to have come directly from the set of the film *Deliverance*, except fatter, and with more tattoos and facial hair.

I struck up a conversation with a tattooed and hirsute couple on a nearby table and learned that Cuba was only a four-hour flight from many places in Canada, so this was their version of Benidorm. Turns out we were surrounded by hicks, hillbillies, and rednecks. Who knew that Canada had them?

At one point I turned to Sally to gauge her demeanour. She had her face raised to the sun. Looking down and meeting my gaze, she smiled and reached out to stroke my bicep. I smiled at her half-heartedly, still unsure of her mood. "Shall we decamp to the beach?"

"Yes, hopefully there will be a better class of people."

There wasn't, but we were treated to a majestic beach, complete with white sand and clear blue-and-green water. We stood on the shore, letting the water lap at our feet, and I grabbed her little finger with my little finger and squeezed. It was time for me to be the peacemaker again. I just couldn't help myself. "Sorry about yesterday. I should have paid more attention to you and listened to what you said. I never meant to hurt you."

She pondered that for a second, her eyes focused on the water, then stared at me. "When you act like that, it makes me feel small and insignificant. My ex, well, let's just say that being faithful wasn't one of his strong points."

I went to ask which one but caught myself. Now wasn't the time for remarks like that. I moved in closer. "You've never told me that before. I'm sorry you had to go through that." I lifted her chin and gazed into her eyes. "I never have and never will cheat on you."

She maintained our eye contact and nodded. "I know." She stroked the side of my face, and the release of tension was palpable.

My legs shook, and I planted my feet more firmly into the ground and exhaled, scanning the sea. "Beautiful, hey?"

"Yeah, I could get used to it. Another drink?"

I nodded. "You make yourself comfortable on a lounger. I'll fetch the drinks."

"Aw, you're so lovely, aren't you, always fetching my drinks, looking after me. You'll always do that, won't you? Look after me?"

Was a life of servitude what lay before me? *No*, I thought, my resistance building. But for now, I'd keep the peace. "Of course I will."

∽

Several mojitos and a change of clothes later, we found ourselves back in the hotel bar waiting for our Christmas Eve gala meal. Sally wore a knee-length blue dress that showed off all her curves. I couldn't keep my eyes off her. "You look stunning, babe."

She ran her hands over it. "This old thing? Had it ages."

I'd put on a nice short-sleeved shirt and a dressy pair of shorts. I waited. And waited. And waited some more. The expected compliment didn't come. My heart sank a little, but I didn't want to fish for one. Instead, I ordered two cocktails.

Time to drown my sorrows.

I hated Christmas; truth be told. Ever since I'd split up with my sons' mum, I'd spent only one Christmas Day with them. I found the entire season painful. Even though my sons were both teenagers now, the pain had never gone away.

By the time the bell rang to announce that the gala meal would be served soon, Sally and I were drunk as skunks and frisky. We followed the crowd to the restaurant, which was situated in another building on the complex, separate from the main hotel building. We left the lobby via the rear exit and headed onto the grounds. "God, I love you," I said, staggering to the right and nearly into a bush. "I want you now."

"Darling, be careful." Sally grabbed me to offer support, but my trajectory and weight pulled us both down, off the path and into the grass, where we missed several thorns and branches by an inch. As I hauled myself on top of Sally in a drunken attempt to mount her, one of the hotel staff appeared.

"Please. I help you." He reached down.

"Don't need your help." I swiped his hand away. A couple more staff appeared. Suddenly there were hands all over me and I was back on my feet. Sally brushed the grass and dirt off her dress. I looked down. My knees were brown. "My knees," I said with a laugh. "Looks like I've been—"

One of the staff bowed and held out his hand. "Excuse me, sir, please, your room number and ticket for the gala evening."

I scrambled around in my pockets and handed him my key and our tickets.

He peeked at them. "Thank you. Come with me." He walked us to the front of the queue outside the restaurant building and then whispered something to the maître'd, who ushered us inside to a table for two near the back, away from the other tables.

"Aw." Sally cocked her head and looked at me. "We've got our own table. We're special, darling. Did you arrange this? How romantic. I love you."

I puffed out my chest. "Yes, yes, I did." *No, no, I didn't.*

"How sweet." She went to stroke my face and missed.

The rest of the evening flashed by in a blur. I do remember that they allowed us more alcohol, but not too much. Whereas they plonked bottles on other tables, they brought us small glasses of rank wine. The food was disgusting and dry.

When Sally went to the toilet, she left her phone. Feeling brave in my inebriation, I picked it up. A message from someone called John flashed up.

Hi how r u hope ur havin a gr8 time xxx

I quickly put down the mobile, and my fuzzy brain tried to comprehend what it had seen. Was this the same John Sally had been seeing when we started dating? Why would he be messaging her? Why three kisses? That seemed pretty forward. He was out of the picture soon after we became a couple. According to her, anyway.

Guilt and shame kicked in. Even as drunk as I was, I knew I shouldn't be reading her messages. I'd vowed never to do that again, after Dawn, yet here I was doing it again. Nearly invoking the nuclear option.

But I couldn't deny that the message spelt danger.

I awoke on Christmas morning with a pounding head and memories of debauchery. As I put the pieces together, I couldn't believe we hadn't been thrown out of the gala dinner—and the hotel. Then I remembered the message I'd seen on Sally's phone and repressed a wave of nausea.

Why was John texting her? Why three kisses? Perhaps she'd replied saying that she was with me and not to message her again. Between the hangover, my confusion over the message, and the usual Christmas Day blues, the day ahead did not feel promising.

I glanced around the room. For a four-star hotel and resort, it was scruffy. A bit of a dump. The paint was peeling, and the furniture was falling apart. The chunky television produced nothing but static. My inspection of the bathroom turned up mould, cracked tiles, and gaps along the skirting board. I thought back to the Nacional de Cuba and wondered if the cockroaches communicated with their friends and family here.

We slowly got ready for breakfast—any sudden movements only exacerbated our hangover-induced pain—and made our way to the lobby. In the reception area, I approached the information desk. "Do you have a map of the resort?"

"No." The receptionist kept her gaze on the screen of her computer from the 1980s.

I persisted. In a country where the customer service was largely non-existent or rubbish, I'd learned not to be put off after the first attempt. "Yeah, so I'm not sure where we're supposed to be eating breakfast and wondered if you had, like, a little fold-up map showing where everything is?"

"Sign outside." She pointed towards the back of the hotel. Her eyes never moved from the computer screen.

"Thank you, you've been most helpful. Have a great day."

Shaking my head, I wandered over to Sally, who was leaning against a fake marble pillar in the middle of the lobby staring down at her phone.

"What's happening?" she asked. "Where's breakfast? Where's the map?"

"There's a sign back here that will answer all our questions." I pointed to the back of the lobby and an exit.

Outside, I couldn't find the mythical signage. The place seemed familiar though . . .

That bush, and to the left, grass and two indents in the lawn.

I glanced down at my knees and had a flashback of clambering on top of Sally. Thank goodness the hotel staff had come along to break up the impromptu show and save me from some embarrassment. At least they didn't know our room number.

"Where's breakfast?" Sally asked again, holding the back of her hand to her head and bending her knees slightly. "I'm feeling faint."

A bit overdramatic, I thought, suppressing an eye roll. In the absence of signs, I tried to remember how we'd got to the restaurant where the gala dinner had been held. I paused to observe several other guests and noticed most seemed to be headed in the same direction. "This way."

"Are you sure?"

"Yeah, 90 per cent." I took her hand, and we followed the crowd. This was like *The Crystal Maze* but without the fun, prizes, and strange bald man.

"Merry Christmas, and happy birthday to our lord and saviour, Jesus Christ," a guest said to me on the way.

"Yeah, erm, you too," I said to the back of his head, suppressing a giggle. I'd stopped observing the religious aspect of Christmas long ago. Then I briefly wondered whether my life would improve if I prayed to our lord and saviour, Jesus Christ. It hadn't exactly been a bed of roses so far.

"Oh, a pool." Sally pointed at it.

Grey foamy flecks had formed on the surface of the green water. Dark patches ran along the pool's edges and bottom. Reminded me of a biology experiment gone wrong. "Not sure about those foamy bits." I wondered if Tyrone had got involved with it. I wouldn't be swimming in that later, that was for sure.

Then Sally tugged on my hand and stopped dead in her tracks. "Where is it? I can't walk any further."

Sometimes being with Sally was like being with an increasingly belligerent toddler. I craned my neck. Up ahead was the restaurant. Thank God. I gestured her forward then sniffed the air and wished I hadn't. Whatever they were cooking smelt less edible than the offering from last night. "Here we are. Told you I was 100 per cent sure it was this way."

"Certain you said 80 per cent."

Inside, I commandeered a table and began my inspection. Benny Hill–style women's uniforms: check. Rude and unhelpful staff: check. Hillbillies: check. Rubbery, tasteless food: check.

At least we had a spectacular beach to enjoy afterwards. We spent the day sunbathing on loungers and gingerly drinking soft drinks and the odd cocktail. We also tried to access the Wi-Fi—I wanted to wish my parents and sons a Merry Christmas—but no luck, despite the hotel's website saying that the signal was supposed to extend this far. I missed them. Here I was, thousands of miles away in a crappy hotel with a woman I no longer trusted and who, I suspected, was lying to others about our relationship and worse.

In an unguarded moment, I felt a familiar feeling of hopelessness smother me to the point where I found it almost difficult to breathe. My shoulders heaved as sobs overtook me.

Sally sat up on her lounger. Concern etched her face. "Darling, what's up?"

The tears continued to flow. The last time I'd cried this

hard was after the most recent break-up with Sally. Sometimes my sensitive soul felt like a curse. "No . . . Noth . . . Nothing."

She swapped over to my lounger and wrapped an arm around my shoulder. "I miss Harry too. It's Christmas Day and we need to be able to contact them. Why don't we go to the main building and see if we can sort out some Wi-Fi? Come on."

In the reception area, I wandered around holding my phone out. Eventually, I got two bars. "Sally, quick, over here. Before it disappears." I planted my feet on the ground and managed to send messages to my sons and parents. My mood lifted, and I smiled for the first time that day.

Then I found an email telling me our booking in the Cayman Islands for 26 December had fallen through. A massive and looming problem. We had flights booked but no place to stay on the Cayman Islands. I scratched my head and told Sally the news.

"What, another booking fell through? Why? Well, book another one." She peered back down at her phone.

Several minutes and many sites later, I'd found nothing. *Crap.* "There's nothing available."

She continued staring at her screen. "Try another site."

"It's the Christmas holidays. There are no vacancies."

"We'll find something when we get there. Simple. Do I have to sort it, like everything else?"

I finally snapped. "You've done nothing! I've booked and sorted out this entire trip!" So much for my plan to take the high and moral ground.

That got her attention. Her head jerked up. "Don't speak to me like that. I . . . I . . . I . . ." She covered her face with her hands and her shoulders moved up and down.

My patience was wearing thin, but I put a hand on her shoulder as guilt nagged away at me. "Sal, listen, I've tried. I can't do any research to see whether it's a good idea to just turn up. What if we go and there're no rooms or hotels we can stay in? What then?"

"We'll sleep on the beach," she said with a shrug.

"Really, Mrs Five-Star Resort?"

"Yeah, why not?"

I took a deep breath. "I'll tell you what's going to happen," I said calmly. "If you want to book a room in the Cayman Islands, go ahead. Be my guest. I'm going to have a walk around Varadero and see if we can find a room here instead. You're more than welcome to join me."

She averted her eyes. "But I can't book the room. You always do that."

At least she was acknowledging it. "Join me. Think of it as a bit of an adventure."

"Oh, you and your stupid adventures. Why can't you be happy with your life?"

Though desperate to throw her words back in her face—*You* wanted the adventure! *You're* unhappy with *your* life! —I held my tongue in a vice-like grip. I held out my hand. "Come. Let's get changed, eat, and go home-hunting."

Sally slouched and pouted. Making clear her unhappiness at our Cayman trip being off. Me? I was relieved. One less travel arrangement to sort out.

"I'll take that as a yes then."

∾

A couple of hours later, we were wandering Varadero trying to find a place to stay.

"Ironic that it's Christmas and we have no place to stay after tonight," I said with a chuckle. "No rooms in the inn. We're just like Mary and Joseph." I peeked at Sally's belly. "You even look pregnant, the bump on you."

"That is so not funny," she snapped. "You know how sensitive I am about my weight. You have a child late in life and see how your body looks afterwards."

"But I love your tubby little belly."

Immediately after I said it, I was shocked by my insensitivity. She pushed me away and stared at me with murderous eyes. Why had I brought up such an explosive issue while matters were so tense? Attempting to keep it all together was proving a greater strain than I'd imagined.

Three hours after beginning our search, we returned to the hotel with no leads. Then an idea popped into my head. My solution was far from ideal, but at this point, I saw no other option. Sally agreed reluctantly when I told her.

I went to the reception desk and waited behind the couple being served. Despite there being six receptionists behind the counter, only one was dealing with guests. When it was my turn, I approached with a big smile. "Hi, how are you this evening?"

She kept her eyes on her computer screen. "What do you want?"

I coughed and scratched my head nervously. "Yeah, so we're due to check out tomorrow and I wanted to see if we could extend our stay at your wonderful hotel?"

The woman didn't move her head, didn't make eye contact. "Room number?" I gave it to her, and she tapped away on her keyboard. "No." She looked up but stared behind me.

I turned around and held back the next person in the queue before facing the receptionist again. "Sorry, no what?"

"No more nights."

Damn. Thwarted again. I was getting seriously worried now. We'd be homeless in a couple of days. How could I tell

Sally this? How would she react? "Oh, okay." I shuffled my feet. "Is it worth checking tomorrow morning?"

She finally looked at me. "No. You're not welcome anymore. You had sex on the grass last night. You no longer stay here." She waved me away.

I gripped the desk. Oh my God. "No. We fell over and your staff helped us up and"—I cleared my throat—"no funny business happened."

"Goodbye. Next."

I trudged back to Sally, my face beetroot red. This was worse than the time we'd crashed the wedding in Margate and got thrown out of the party. Now we were being thrown out of the hotel, kind of, and for . . . indecent behaviour. The shame!

"Well?"

I stared down at my feet. "They won't let us extend our stay."

"Why?" she asked, waving her arms about. "Don't they have rooms? Can't imagine a place like this would be fully booked, Christmas or not."

I swayed from side to side, struggling to make eye contact with her. "The issue is that they won't let us because of the incident last night."

"What incident?"

"When we rolled about on the grass and I was on top of you."

"What! So, your fault. AGAIN." She turned her back on me.

"Hang on a minute," I said, straightening. "You were involved too, remember."

She swivelled round. "Well, I didn't give them our room number. Did you?"

"Not that I can . . . Oh wait, they asked for our gala ticket and . . ." I slapped my forehead. "I showed them that and our key, which had the number on it."

"IDIOT. Why did you do that?"

"I was drunk, so were you. Look, none of this is helping us get a room and I'm starving and not eating here." I rubbed my belly. "We passed a place when we were looking for somewhere to stay. A Chinese restaurant, I think. Let's go there."

She grudgingly agreed, and we headed to our room via the back of the hotel, but as we turned a corner, we almost crashed into the guard who stood in our way. "No." He pointed back to the hotel.

I pointed behind him. "But our room is just there. I can see the block. It's less than a minute away."

"No. Hotel." He continued to point in the direction from which we had come. I took a step forward; he reached for his walkie-talkie. Was he going to call for help, hit me with it, or summon the police? Anybody's guess.

Sally shoved me aside. "This is ridiculous." He moved to stand in front of Sally. Whichever direction she moved, he mirrored her movement and blocked her path. Now, I played British Bulldog as a kid, so I knew the tactics. The key one being that the ticker could only tick one person at a time. There were two of us. I could make it to the apartment, but that wouldn't help Sally, and the hotel already saw us as trouble. I certainly had no desire to see us thrown out early.

I took Sally's arm and pulled her towards me. "Come on, let's go back."

"Stupid man." She stared at him.

"Yes, he is, but I don't want any more hassles."

"You're so soft, Kevin. You need to harden up." She was right, but not in the way she imagined. I needed to harden up in my dealings with her—and I wasn't talking about sex.

It took us a quarter of an hour to get back to our room the long way, through the main hotel building, and our mutual tension and frustration increased exponentially. There had once been a period in my life when I had no home to call my own, following my split from my ex-wife. I sofa-surfed and stayed in hotels until I found my own place to rent. It was a dark and distressing time in my life, and today had been triggering unpleasant memories of it.

A quick change of clothes and a short walk later, we sat down to eat in what turned out to be a palatable state-run Chinese restaurant called Lai Lai. The server was wearing the obligatory Benny Hill uniform, except she'd added her own touch: cycling shorts under the skirt. We ate in silence, but the decent food helped my brain to function—that and removing myself from the stress bucket and pressure cooker that was the hotel.

After paying for our meal, I stood. "Come on, let's go back. I think I've figured out how we're going to get a room."

17

LAST ROOM AT THE INN

My head thudded and my stomach churned. After my big plan to get a room—trying to extend our stay at the hotel—by drunkenly complaining to the manager—had failed, I'd spent the rest of the evening drowning my sorrows and watching Sally flirt with the male staff in the hotel bar. Lovely.

Now, in the light of the morning, I was smacked in the face by the realisation that after tonight we had nowhere to stay until New Year's Eve. My brain ticked, trying to grasp at a solution. I grabbed my phone off the nightstand. No signal. Surprise, surprise.

I got up, and after a fruitless attempt to access the internet in the lobby, I returned to the room to find Sally still asleep. Noticing her phone light up, I crept over to her side of the bed and spied another message on her phone from John.

Miss and luv u loads xxx

Nausea pushed up through my throat, and I steadied myself against the wall. Voices vied for attention in my head: *She's cheating on you! No, they're just friends!*

Several more messages fought their way through. *The internet must work intermittently*, I thought. I went to grab the mobile, but Sally stirred. I stepped away as she opened her eyes.

Spotting her phone coming to life, she turned it, so the screen was facing downwards. Her brow furrowed. "Where have you been?"

"To reception, to sort out some Wi-Fi."

She sat up. "Any luck?"

"No," I said, pacing back and forth.

"What are you going to do?"

I needed to leave the room and process what I'd just seen. "Me," I said, shoving a digit in my solar plexus, "I'm going to eat breakfast. Pack up. Check out. Leave our bags here. Head to the internet shop to buy some vouchers and take it from there. What about you?"

She yawned and lay back down. "Ten more minutes in bed, maybe wander down for some food."

"No ideas about how to sort this out?"

"Your department, darling."

I clenched my fists to repress the scream of frustration that wanted to escape.

Over breakfast, I mulled over the situation. The evidence was piling up—Sally had either never ended her relationship with John, or it had been re-consummated. Either way, it was disastrous for me. I'd vowed not to make excuses for her anymore, and I wasn't sure I even could at this point. But I didn't know if I could face the issue yet. The thought of dealing with it in the here and now made me feel shaky.

I decided to bide my time. It was the only decision I could make in the moment. I returned to the room to find Sally packing.

"Any news?" she asked, folding a T-shirt.

"No, I came back to check on you, see if you were awake."

"I am. Now what?"

"How about you pack, and I'll wait for you in the lobby?" I said, still needing some distance.

Annoyance flashed across her face. "What, all your stuff as well?"

I shook my head. "Already done." I picked up my backpack and heaved it onto my back. "Meet you in reception."

"But what about me?"

"You're an adult. Clean up your own mess." I stalked out and found myself in a familiar scene: a place with disinterested employees and non-existent Wi-Fi. "Goddammit," I said aloud, looking at my phone.

"Hey, my friend. What's up?"

I turned to see a staff member Sally had been flirting with, in the bar the previous night. *Great.* I waved my phone in the air. "This internet isn't working."

"Can I help you?"

This was the friendliest any of the staff in the hotel had been. Normally, I found asking for help tortuous. I'd rather stew. But today, my predicament trumped my discomfort. I nodded and blurted it all out. "My girlfriend and I are due to go to the Cayman Islands, but we can't because we have no accommodation and I've been trying to get online to find a place here and I can't because of the stupid Wi-Fi not working and last night we went around to hotels and casas to find a place but everywhere was booked up and now we're going to be homeless and I just want somewhere to stay and I don't know what I'm going to do." I slumped against a pillar and let out a deep breath.

"Okay," he said, unfazed. "I might be able to help. I have a friend. Meet me here at eleven." Before I could properly express my gratitude, he smiled and walked away.

Sally turned up in the hotel lobby at 10.55 looking mean and moody. I checked us out and then exchanged some more money. The robbing bastard of a hotel used a different exchange rate. Elsewhere, the rate was 1 pound for 1.44 Cuban dollars. Here it was 1.22.

"So, you sorted anything yet?" she asked. "Plus, I need to

access my messages." Before my rage could take shape again, my new friend reappeared.

"Hey, my friend." He nodded at me. When Sally caught his eye, he smiled nervously.

"Hi," Sally said, linking her arm through mine and looking at me with a similar nervous smile. "You two know each other?"

"Yeah, we got talking earlier on. He's trying to help us." Their nervousness made me twitchy and suspicious. Had she been out of my sight last night? Perhaps, but not that long, I don't think.

He half-turned and ushered us to follow. "Come with me."

I stepped forward then halted as memories of Marrakesh assaulted me. "Whoa hang on. Where are we going?"

"Please. Come. My friend Julia, lives nearby. We go now."

My legs moved but my guard was up. I'd trust him one step at a time.

As soon as we left the hotel, the heavens opened, but our new guide strode ahead, and any thoughts of waiting it out evaporated. My guard hadn't been ready for this particular eventuality. Within seconds, my clothes were soaked. Sally emitted screeches and squeals, and her face was as thunderous as the skies. I ignored her. We walked for ten minutes along the road from the hotel into a residential area. The sky flashed with lightning. We passed a dead cat.

It all felt rather apocalyptic.

Feeling like a drowned rat, I stood next to Sally on the pavement as our friend approached a house and knocked. An olive-skinned woman with red hair opened the door, and after they'd spoken briefly, we were introduced.

"Hello," Julia said with a warm smile. "I promise you I will find you a place. So sad, no place to live."

"Bye, my friend," said our guide. "And good luck."

"Thank you." I reached into my pocket.

"No, my friend. Not necessary." He waved and ran quickly

back towards the hotel. Overwhelmed by his kindness, I felt a tear trickle down my cheek amidst the rain. He'd had no reason to help us, but he'd done it anyway.

Julia guided us under the cover of her porch, and a child brought us each a bottle of water. He grinned as he skipped away then jumped and giggled as thunder exploded overhead.

"My hero," Sally said, snuggling close, "finding us a place to stay. I love you."

I closed my eyes. "Yes, I know." But did she also love John? John, who missed and loved Sally? Who was still on the scene? My competitive spirit reared its head. Right now, Sally was sitting with me, in Cuba. I needed to show her I was the better man for her. And I'd start by finding us a place to stay.

The torrential downpour became a trickle. As a beam of sunlight pierced the clouds, Julia appeared in her front door. "Good news," she said, beaming. "I found you a place. Please come with me. I'll take you there." She stepped down from the porch and headed towards the gate, ushering us to follow.

The clearing of the weather and Julia's good news lifted my figurative dark clouds. A change of fortune, perhaps? I strapped on my backpack.

"Is it far?" Sally asked, standing.

"No, a ten-minute walk," Julia said.

Sally turned to me and bent backwards slightly, holding her lower back. "Babe, my back is sore. Can you carry my bag?"

I grabbed it and muttered to myself as she walked away.

"You're the best," she called, following Julia.

I blew air out of my mouth. "Yeah, right."

"Tonight, you stay in this apartment," Julia explained, as I caught them up, panting. "And tomorrow I meet you at eleven and take you to another place nearby."

I smiled through gritted teeth, the bags weighing me down. "Amazing. Thank you. I can't thank you enough."

Sally touched my arm and lowered her eyebrows. "Steady on, you've thanked her enough."

I glared at her. My dark clouds were back.

At our new casa, Julia introduced us to Sophia, a young Cuban woman. She showed us to a room up a flight of stairs, and I dumped the bags immediately and bent over to catch my breath.

Despite my back being saturated with sweat, I couldn't help but smile as I looked around. Along with a bedroom and a shower, we also had a dining room, a living room, and a balcony. I glanced at Sally, who nodded, clearly impressed. I breathed a sigh of relief. I'd needed this victory.

As Julia went to leave, I hugged her and pulled a few notes out of my wallet. But when I handed them to her, she threw them to the ground. *Oh no. Did I insult her?*

Then she picked up the cash and put it into Sally's hand. "Please. No money. I am glad you stay here."

She'd gone way out of her way to help and wanted nothing in return. It just went to show that there were all kinds of people in every country. I was grateful to have met a few of the kind ones in Cuba today.

I headed to the balcony and saw a crowd gathering in the casa's courtyard, Sophia among them. Music blared, and cans of lager and bottles of rum were stacked on a table.

"Looks like a party," Sally said, coming up beside me. "Shall we join them?"

I stretched my back. "Why not?" Then I remembered the last party we'd gate-crashed—the wedding reception, in Margate. There was the raid on the sweets table, the near fight with the couple over spilt drinks, the ignominy of being asked to leave . . .

Was this such a good idea?

At the bottom of the stairs, a large Cuban man with greying hair surrounding a bald spot blocked our path and grinned. "Hey, you come to join our party. Please come, my friends."

Another friend. What a day this was turning out to be. He held out his hands. I went to shake one of them, but he pulled me in for a hug that lasted six seconds. I know because I counted. Sally smirked at me and wandered off.

I coughed and caught my breath. "You speak fantastic English."

"I am an American citizen," he said proudly and loudly. "Me and my family, we are originally from Cuba, but now we are American."

"I'm Kevin."

"Tony."

We moved away from the stairs and into the courtyard. "Are you allowed back in Cuba?"

"Am I not here?" He looked down at the spot on which he stood.

"Yeah, but I thought Cuba and America were sworn enemies."

"Yes, but now relations are loosening, like they had a few rums"—he mimicked drinking from glasses, knocking one back from each hand—"and getting to understand each other a little and finding they like each other a little."

I'd never heard international relations compared to inebriation, but the analogy worked. "So, everyone here is from America?" I said, gesturing to the courtyard.

"No. You know my niece." He pointed towards Sophia. "And her parents, brothers, sisters—all their family is here."

I adjusted my footing, so I was facing him. Finally, someone, I could talk to about the country. "Is it easy to travel between the two countries now?"

"Difficult, but easier, yes. Here, my friend, your hand is

empty." He waved to a young man and gestured. The guy ran over with two beers and handed me one.

I smiled gratefully, tugged back the ring pull, and took a swig. Nothing like the bliss of the first cold beer on a hot day. I held it up to him. "Thank you, very kind of you." I took another sip and a few more. It tasted amazing, Cristal, I think, and its after-effects squeezed the remaining stress from my body. I didn't know where Sally was, and in that moment, I didn't care. "Was it easy for you to become an American citizen?"

"We were all dry feet," he said and slurped his beer.

I furrowed my brow and squinted at him.

He explained. "In America, the policy is that if they catch you at sea, wet feet, they send you back to Cuba. We made the shore, not captured like the stupid ones, and after many years we became American citizens."

"Great for you. How come your family here doesn't go to America?" I peered around at the assembled partygoers.

"Dangerous still, and my brother, he is getting old. My niece and nephews stay, to care for their relations. Perhaps one day they will go to America." He gazed over at them, his face mournful.

I shuffled on the spot a little. Time to bring out the big questions. "So . . . what do you think about Cuba, Fidel, and communism?"

"I went away. That tells you everything you need to know. There is nothing here. In America, great opportunities, plenty of everything."

"But you're here now. That must mean something?"

"Yes, some of my relations are here, and family is especially important to Cuban people." He finished his beer and placed the can on a wall. "I love them, and I want the best for them."

"But why did you leave in the first place? Was it risky for you?" I considered the effort it had taken just to persuade me to travel abroad again. I couldn't imagine moving overseas and living in a different culture. I admired his courage.

"Back then and even now, difficult to be yourself here. You must be who the government and the party officials want you to be. I couldn't stand living a lie anymore, so I escaped."

Sally appeared at my side. "What are you up to?"

I smiled at her, but I was more interested in my conversation with Tony. In doing something for me. "Talking to my new friend Tony about America, Cuba, Fidel, politics—the usual party stuff."

She looked at my hand. "Where did you get that beer?"

"Here, sweetheart," Tony shouted to a different young lad, who quickly approached with three beers and handed them out. I knocked back my first beer and placed the empty next to Tony's.

"Thank you," Sally said, taking a sip. "Oh, ice cold. Hmm, lovely." She wiped her mouth with her hand then wandered off and started talking to a handsome, bare-chested man who sported an eight-pack. Typical Sally. I fought back the urge to march over and break up her little tête-à-tête before refocusing on the conversation I was enjoying.

Tony nudged me. "Your wife?" He pointed a large finger towards her. "I see no ring."

I shook my head. "No, my girlfriend."

He nodded, took out a fat cigar from a packet in the top pocket of his shirt, and offered one to me.

"No, thanks." I didn't normally smoke, and I had a specific idea in mind for the cigars I'd bought for my dad and sons. A photo of the four of us, pretending to smoke them.

He bit off the end and lit it, took a long drag, and blew the smoke out. "She reminds me of my first love. Exquisite, but dangerous. You be careful, my friend. A woman like that attracts many men and sometimes is hard for them to say no. If you understand my drift."

I spied the scene. The guy's hand was now around her

waist, and her hand was on his bare shoulder. I nodded. "Yeah, you might be right."

"What do you mean? Tony is always right. Yes?"

I chuckled. "Of course."

"Why are you here?"

"Long story, my friend."

He gazed around. "You have somewhere else to go? Something to do. We have time."

I smiled. That we did. The Cubans' concept of time was completely different from the one I was accustomed to. In London, I was always rushing to and from work, Sally's, meet-ups, and events. Everything was planned out, to the point where I had no time for myself. Here, time was to be savoured. It unfolded without plans, without diaries, without alarms. I loved this aspect of Cuban culture.

The next morning, Sally and I stood in the casa's courtyard, which was littered with remnants of the festivities. Meanwhile, my mind was littered with remnants of my conversation with Tony. His first love, the one he'd compared to Sally, had been unfaithful to him and broken his heart. "Either marry her or dump her," he'd advised me. Not clear on why I had to make that choice, I asked him to elaborate.

Marriage, he'd explained, would make her think twice before being unfaithful, and she'd be less likely to run off. I wasn't sure Tony's advice transferred to British culture. I got the feeling that Cubans held marriage vows dearer than we did.

One thing was for sure: the Cubans knew how to party. Sally and I had staggered up to our room around midnight, and the noise had finally died down at about three in the morning.

Bleary-eyed, I handed our room key to Sophia when she approached us in the courtyard. "Thanks again. The apartment was beautiful." I spotted Julia at the entrance chatting to a passer-by.

"Thank you," Sophia said. "I hope you enjoy your stay in the next casa."

"Do you know the owners?"

She nodded. "He is a cousin of my mother."

Taking a stab at another quick conversation with a local, I asked, "So is this your full-time job, managing the casa?"

"Yes."

"What did you do before?"

"I was a pharmacist, but this pays better."

Wow. "Was that not a well-paid job here?"

"No, my father was making more for renting out an apartment for one night than I earned in a month."

I'd paid thirty-five bucks for the night—more than we'd paid for our rooms in Cienfuegos and Trinidad, but not by much. Striking, how tourism lured educated professionals to the industry. But at what cost to the overall Cuban economy. I wondered. I'd thought socialism was about curing the ills of the market, but this seemed topsy-turvy. "Well, thanks again, and have a wonderful rest of your life."

She laughed. "Thank you. You too."

"Have a wonderful rest of your life," Sally said, mimicking my voice—a difficult feat, considering its deepness. "Can't remember you saying that to Yari or Ruth." I hadn't, because they didn't speak English. But I knew what she was hinting at. "Did you think she was beautiful?"

And there it was. Yes, Sophia's stunning beauty had mesmerised me. But I'd learned from my previous mistake. "No, not at all. Nowhere near as beautiful as you, anyway." I should have left my comments there, but I got carried away and added, "God, no, she was a right minger. Definitely hit with the ugly stick when she was born."

Sally just pursed her lips and shook her head. Damned if I did and damned if I didn't.

Julia escorted us to our new casa, which was a fifteen-minute walk away, and introduced us to the owner, Paul, a larger-than-life character with a booming voice. The accommodation was nowhere as luxurious as the previous one, but it was ours till we moved back to Havana. Our room was one in a row of rooms on either side of a narrow passageway. Still, I was grateful. We thanked Julia once again, jettisoned our bags, and headed out to explore.

I stared up at the sky and noticed the clouds rolling in. "Doesn't look like beach weather to me." I nodded towards a bright yellow vehicle. "There's one of the tourist buses—shall we hop on?"

"Might as well," Sally said with a sigh.

I bit back my frustration. Her lack of enthusiasm grated on me. Yet again, I was the one figuring out how to make the day fun.

The first level of the bus was packed, so we headed up to the less busy, open-top level. The vehicle set off, leaning to one side—the side we were sitting on. I'd put on some weight, but not that much, surely? We swapped over to seats on the other side of the aisle, but that didn't help the issue. Fantastic for my self-confidence, less so for my anxiety about the bus keeling over.

Want to know how to spend a tedious day in Varadero? Go on a tour. One tourist complex was modelled on a marina. That was about as interesting as the trip got. The guide informed us about every resort and hotel we passed. And she ended every sentence with a singsong "Varadero". At first, I was in fits of giggles over it. But after the hundredth time—and that is not an exaggeration—my mood shifted. In my head, I imagined standing in front of her, pointing a gun in her face, and shouting, "Say 'Varadero' again—I dare you!"

My dark fantasy was interrupted by a rainstorm. Sally and

I hastened to the bottom level for cover and squeezed in with everyone else.

After returning to our Casa following the tour, we spent the evening eating and drinking before retiring to bed early. The stress, and emotions, having caught up with me and my need to sleep overwhelming.

One thing Varadero had in abundance was small markets. That day, we explored all of them, much to Sally's delight. The relief of having our accommodation sorted until we got to Havana had lifted an enormous weight off my shoulders, so I happily indulged Sally in her shopping. After all, keeping her happy was the whole point of this trip.

Many of the stalls were lined with vividly coloured paintings, magic boxes, and two-pound bottles of rum, along with the obligatory Che Guevara T-shirts. Every stall had them.

"Oh, babe," Sally said, pointing. "Is that a newsagent or a bookshop or something?" She walked towards it.

I squinted. "Won't be a newsagent. More likely a bookshop."

She hurried her pace. "I bet you I could buy magazines, catch up on all my celebrity gossip."

"I doubt that very much." We entered the store, and I couldn't help but smirk. It was full of books about Che Guevara, Fidel Castro, and the virtues of Marxism-Leninism. I picked up a few and smelt them. I'd always loved the feel and smell of old hardbacks. My heaven and Sally's hell.

"Darling, what is all this nonsense?" she said, picking up several books then tossing them aside. "Is this what you used to read?"

"Well, I have read books on Cuba and Marxism-Leninism, but not nowadays." I stroked the books as I strolled past them.

"So, you were a proper commie."

"Left-wing, yes, but not a commie."

"Ooooh, who's this handsome devil?" Thinking she meant me, I blushed. Then I spotted the picture of Che Guevara she was staring at. "My God, he's gorgeous, this bloke."

You've got to be kidding. Now I was competing with Che?

She glanced out of the window. "Right, I think I've seen some stalls selling bongos."

"Bongos?" I said, following her out of the shop. "For Harry?"

"No, not Harry. I want to buy one for a friend."

"Which friend?"

"Oh, no one you know."

My suspicions aroused; I felt my hackles rise.

"Hmm," she said, perusing the offerings and occasionally trying them out. There were quite a few stalls selling bongos. It was a bit of a thing here. "I'm looking for an excellent quality one. My friend is a semi-professional player."

I scoffed. "Is that even a thing?"

"Yes, and don't make fun," she snapped.

I chewed on my nail, caught myself, and stopped. "So, who is this friend?"

She picked up a bongo, weighing it in her hand. "I've told you—you don't know them. I don't know all your friends." She tapped her fingers on it and put it down.

I picked it up and rapped it with my hand. "You do, but to be fair, there's not a lot of them."

She whirled around. "What does it matter to you?"

"Curious why you're making such a tremendous fuss over buying a bongo for a friend. How much are you looking to spend?" *And why are you so defensive about this mystery friend?*

She turned away. "Not sure. Fifty perhaps."

My head jolted upwards, and my stomach flipped. "Fifty what? Pence? Dollars? Pounds?"

"Pounds."

"Hell of a mate you got there. Must be your best pal ever

for that amount of money." Throughout the trip, we'd bought a few little things for Harry and cigars for my family, but nothing for anyone else. I crossed my arms. "Who is he?"

She faced me. "Stop. You don't know him. Why are you making such a huge thing? It's got nothing to do with you."

So, I was right. It was a him. My face flushed, and I couldn't stop my body from shaking. "Go on. I'll leave you to it. I'll be over there." I stalked off and pretended to be interested in a stall selling wooden carvings. Meanwhile, my head was in turmoil. Who was he? It had to be John. A thousand other questions spun around in my head. I remembered my conversation with Jenny. I needed to investigate more, find proof of Sally's unfaithfulness.

Five minutes later, Sally joined me. "Well, that's spoilt my day. I want to go home." She turned around and hailed a metallic pink Cadillac convertible.

Once we were seated, she began recording a video of the inside of the car. I leant in to photobomb it. She moved away from me, but I reckoned I got my ugly mug in the shot. Why was she trying to keep me out of the video? I thought about her refusal to accept my friend request on Facebook. Did she really post about us?

And was that the least of my worries, considering all the other information stacking up?

18

PURPLE GIRAFFE

"I wish you had a unique name."

I sucked my piña colada through my straw. "Which one? Kevin or Kelly?"

After returning to our casa, where Sally and I crossed paths with another partying Cuban family—they'd invited us to join but we'd declined, still feeling the effects of the night before—we'd enjoyed a lovely meal in the front garden watching Cuban life pass us by. Sonia, our octogenarian host, both cooked and served it, we assumed. The food was out of this world, and I told her so. Home-made tomato soup was followed by chicken and fried rice with mushrooms and prawns.

Though the meal was fantastic, I hadn't been able to shake my pensive mood. My mind kept wandering to the bongo incident, and I couldn't separate facts from perceptions. My desire to confront Sally was tempered by my fear of how we'd get through the rest of the vacation and travel back to London together.

Now, Sally and I were sipping cocktails at a place called the Purple Giraffe. An interesting place with an interesting owner. He'd introduced himself and his family right after we were seated. Alfredo had a beautiful wife and daughter, yet all the waitstaff were young men with blond highlights and buff bodies wearing pink polo shirts and tight trousers. Alfredo appeared to admire them as Sally did Luther.

Not long after we'd secured our table, a queue formed on the startlingly white steps to the open-concept rooftop area. Smooth music drifted in the background. Above, the stars twinkled. It was as romantic as anyone could imagine. Too bad the tension between Sally and me was still thick.

"Both," Sally said, in answer to my question about my name. She stirred her cocktail, also a large piña colada.

I imitated her action. "Why?"

"Well, Kevin is a name for losers and weirdos. Wasn't he a hamster or something on a children's television show?" She pushed her straw aside and gulped her piña colada.

I bristled. "Gerbil. Kevin was a gerbil." Kevin the Gerbil. A name that had stuck with me through school and work. Then I straightened. "'Kevin' and 'Kelly' are both Irish names, and together they mean 'handsome warrior'."

Sally laughed, and some of her booze spurted from her mouth. "You're joking. You make me laugh sometimes."

Typical Sally compliment—wrapped in barbed wire.

"Well, your name isn't much better."

She placed her glass back on the table none too gently. "What do you mean?"

"*Coronation Street*? Sally Webster?" I swigged back some drink, also eschewing the straw. "Not winning at the name game, are you, babes?"

She eyed me. "You're getting brave. But you're not exactly a warrior, are you?"

I leant across the table. "I'm a lover, not a fighter."

She smirked. "Don't flatter yourself." She had a point. Physical intimacy had featured little during this trip. She poked the ice in her drink. "What's your middle name?"

"John." I watched her carefully.

Her lip curled. "Nah, can't use that name."

I raised an eyebrow. "Why?"

"Too confusing."

"Why?"

"Well, I was seeing someone with that name when you and I started going out, remember?"

"How could I forget?" I stroked the side of my glass and took a deep breath, trying to maintain my composure. "Yeah, let's stick with Kevin."

She poked her straw toward me. "Give me time and I'll pick out a new name. One more suitable. One that gives you some gravitas."

"You do that." No way was I ditching my name. I might or might not be a loser, but Kevin was my name, and I wore it proudly.

I caught sight of Alfredo sat at the bar, surveying his kingdom and keeping an eye on all his waiters. I nodded towards him. "Do you think he's gay?"

Sally followed my gaze and screwed up her face. "Yes." She turned away and huffed. "People like that annoy the hell out of me."

I frowned. "What, gay people?"

"No, not gay people. People who say they're one thing and then live a lie. He's obviously gay, yet he pretends he's a happily married man. He's going to hurt the people who love him. Selfish prick. I hate people like that." She took a hard swig of her drink and slammed the empty glass down on the table.

Sally's vehemence took me aback. Was it directed at me? Couldn't be. After all, it seemed as though she was the one harbouring deep secrets. So, what had got her so riled up? Had observing Alfredo felt like looking in a mirror? Were her comments actually aimed at herself? I could only speculate, as she quickly changed the subject.

The next morning, to no one's surprise, Sally was insistent on getting some Wi-Fi. First, we headed across the road to a cafe and ordered egg on toast. Sally was particular about her eggs: sunny side up but splashed, so they were runny but the film over the yolk was white. How the hell was I supposed to explain that to the chef in the dirty white apron who didn't speak a word of English?

Stood in the open kitchen, he had his hand on a greasy frying pan. I called to him, and he peered at me. I pointed to the eggs in the frying pan and held my hand out, palm up. Then I flipped my hand over and flipped it back up again, quickly. He imitated the action then flipped the eggs over. I mimed again, and he flipped them again. Sweating like a pig, I gave him a thumbs up. That was hard work.

When the eggs were ready, I took our plates back to our table and laid Sally's in front of her.

She wriggled her nose. "These are runny, babe. Can you ask him to do them a little longer?" She pushed the plate back towards me.

Normally, I would have done her bidding. Today, I sat down, sliced my eggs in half, and watched excitedly as the yellow yolk ran slowly across the toast and onto my plate. "You do that. I'm eating." I cut off a slice of egg and toast and shoved it in my mouth. A little of the yolk ran out of the side of my mouth and onto my chin.

She pulled a face. "What's got into you today? All moody."

I mopped my lips and chin with my fingers. "I'm fine, but I'm starving, and I had to improve my mime skills to ninja-level to make sure he splashed your eggs. I don't know what else to say to him. You have a try instead of criticising all the time."

"All right, I will, no need to be like that." She snatched her plate and stood.

I sighed and almost rose to take over, but a voice in my head said, *sit down and enjoy your breakfast*. That voice showed up now and then. Today I listened to it.

Sally returned to the table empty-handed, and minutes later, the cook loomed large over us. He tossed down the plate with two slimy eggs on toast. The yolk was unsplashed. Sally eyeballed me. I just shrugged, and she tentatively cut away the bits she didn't want, with much muttering.

Afterwards, we made our way up the main street to the Wi-Fi shop, which turned out to be a kiosk. The signal was available only in a small—and I mean tiny—shopping area, which consisted of two shops, a counter selling drinks, and three tables. Sally sat at a table with the voucher while I attempted to buy two beers. "Dos Cristal, por favor." I was really getting a handle on the language.

"No Cristal."

I peered behind the vendor and saw a fridge stuffed full of beer. "Cristal." I pointed at it.

He stared at them and turned back to me. "No Cristal."

"How much?" I pulled some cash out of my wallet, thinking some tourist dollars would assist the transaction. But he was having none of it.

"No Cristal."

I ended up buying a more expensive lager then watched in confusion as he sold a local some Cristal. So much for getting the hang of the language around here.

I returned to Sally and handed her a bottle. She took it and placed it on the table, not looking up, engrossed in her mobile. I perched next to her and snooped over her shoulder. She was typing a message. I noticed the name at the top of her screen: Roger.

Nightmare. I'm scared and wish I were home, sharing a bottle of wine with you xx

What the hell? Before I had time to process that, a

message from John flashed up.

Hey babes, miss u and can't wait 2 c u when u come home, can't believe u gone on your own luv u xxx

Then she switched off her phone and clinked her bottle of beer with mine. "Cheers," she said, seemingly unaware of my nosiness.

"Cheers," I said dully.

"Oh, you're not in one of them dreary moods, are you?" she said, slumping. "Come on, we're on holiday in Cuba. Cheer up."

I nodded. But not in agreement with Sally. I'd made another connection. The puzzle pieces were forming a clear shape of what was going on. And the pressure on me to confront her was growing.

That evening, we took our dinner in the front garden of the host's home again. And again, Sonia's cooking was magnificent.

"Thank you, Sonia," I said, as she cleared away our dishes. "That meal was delicious."

She blushed and smiled.

"Lovely food," Sally said.

Sonia's smile widened and filled her entire face. She disappeared into the house and returned with two more beers for us.

Sally sat up. "Shall we go out tonight?"

"Where?" I swigged back some beer. With the trust between us gone, Sally appeared to be a different woman to me now. Almost a stranger. All I wanted was to go off and do my own thing, but I didn't want to arouse suspicion, given that I hadn't figured out how to handle matters yet.

"Find a bar nearby?" She pointed in the general direction of the main road.

"What, the Purple Giraffe again?"

"No, somewhere else. Must be other bars?"

"I don't know, babe. Not sure this is a bar and club type of place." Really, I just didn't have the energy to watch her flirt or go off with another man tonight.

"Calle 62," boomed a voice to my right. I looked over to see Paul clambering onto his cycle, which had been hitched to the front gate. "It's a good place to go—music, dancing, drinks. And both locals and tourists." Then he rode off into the night, to make some more deals no doubt. I'd noticed various locals coming to the house with wood and scrap metal and leaving various items, including a dress on one occasion and what looked like earphones on another.

A kid approached and also got onto a cycle.

"I've seen a lot of those," I said, pointing to it. "Are they Cuban?"

The kid—well, more a teenager on the verge of adulthood—shook his head. "No, Chinese. They sold us loads of them years ago. Everyone has one."

"Interesting. I'm Kevin. This is my girlfriend, Sally."

"Hi," she said, disinterested.

"I'm Emilio. Paul's nephew."

"Do you live here?"

"Yes, I have one room back there, the one opposite you, I think."

I detected an accent. "You've lived in America, I'm guessing?"

"No."

"Your English is excellent, though."

"A man, he sells tapes with British programmes on them. *Doctor Who* and *Britain's Got Talent* are my favourites."

I smiled inwardly. Despite decades of communist rule, criminal activity still existed here. In the UK a few years earlier, DVD sellers would approach people in shopping centres, trying to entice them to buy their cheap, poor-quality-copy DVDs created with handheld camcorders snuck into cinemas. I hoped the copies here were of better quality than the fuzzy, shaky ones we had at home.

Sonia peered out to make sure we had everything we needed then disappeared back into the house. "I have to say, Emilio, your auntie is an amazing chef. The meals here are fantastic."

He stared at me and then laughed. "She doesn't cook, and she's not family either. She works for us."

"What, like a servant?"

"I don't know the translation."

"But she doesn't cook?"

"No, she serves it. My aunt cooks, and she's amazing at it."

The news devastated me. Seems I couldn't trust anyone these days. Sonia appeared and took away the tablecloth. "Must have taken you hours to prepare such a delicious meal?" I said, my words drenched in sarcasm.

She smiled and nodded.

You lying hag.

"Why are you being a dick?" Sally said, finally joining the conversation. "You know she didn't cook the meal."

Emilio looked back and forth between Sally and me as we spoke, seemingly fascinated by our conversation.

"Because she's a liar."

"No, she isn't. She never said she cooked. You assumed."

"What, you didn't assume as well?"

"Yeah, but so what? She never lied. Get over yourself. Your fault for thinking she did."

"But I thanked her."

"Whatever, this conversation is boring me."

What next? I thought. *Santa Claus claiming he brings the presents? The Tories taking credit for reducing the deficit?* We lived in a world of liars, and Sonia was their queen.

What did that make Sally?

19

LAST-NIGHT SHITE

The next morning, I lay on the bed ruminating while Sally showered. I'd persuaded her not to go to Calle 62 the previous night. "We'll go tomorrow," I'd said, against my better judgement.

Throughout the trip, as I'd run around after Sally, making her happiness my highest priority and failing at every turn, I'd come to realise something: My relationship with her didn't need fixing. It needed to be over. There was nothing else I could do. Cuba, in its inimitable way, had shown me the malaise and rot at the heart of our bond.

I'd come to believe that unless I was needed by her, I had little or no self-worth. I'd lost sight of myself and my purpose—friendships, interests, and values, all cast aside in pursuit of Sally. My desires and needs had become unimportant. I'd stopped articulating them to her, for fear of upsetting and losing her. And so, happiness eluded me.

Why the hell was I staying in a relationship in which the other party didn't want to be associated with me? In which the other party was having an affair?

That thought made my chest tighten.

I was with someone I loved but who might not love me.

Someone whose actions and words consistently inflicted emotional pain. Someone who didn't respect me. But why should she, when I didn't love and respect myself?

I couldn't change Sally, but I could transform myself. This was the difficulty I now faced. I had to deal with what I had become. And the thought of leaving the relationship and tackling my own issues left me feeling nauseous and frightened to my core.

I'd built an identity around sacrificing my needs for hers. And not for the first time in a relationship. That old emotional wound within me was still raw and festering. History had repeated itself, but it was time to face the difficult road and do what needed to be done.

It was time to fix me, and how I related to myself.

Why did the chicken cross the road?

Because this is Cuba. It refuses to follow the instructions of an English imperialist. Recalcitrant bird.

Sally and I were wandering, and I was trying to capture a photo of a chicken so I could post it on my social media accounts with some witty remark about chickens and crossings of roads. Every time I didn't have my phone readily available, the beady-eyed little shit would cross the road.

When I had my mobile ready, the bird just stared at me, mocking me. I tried to take a lesson from it. In life, travel, and relationships, patience is key. Wait and the right moment will come.

I gave up.

"Sunbathing?" I asked, turning to Sally. At least the weather was cooperating. The mid-morning sun was out, and there were only a few clouds in the sky.

"Okay."

We soon discovered a spotless beach with crystal-clear water. I found two sunbeds and was rearranging them when a short bloke with big, flappy ears appeared. "You stay hotel?" he asked while looking at my wrists for non-existent bands.

Trying to navigate Cuban society was a Herculean task. I never knew what kind of response I'd elicit from the locals. Helpful or unhelpful? Polite or rude? Friendly or downright belligerent?

"No," I said cautiously. What reaction was I in store for? "Why? Are these for hotel guests only?" I dropped them, lest I be charged for them. Or arrested.

"Beds for guests, not you." He tugged them away.

Unhelpful, then. "How much?"

He peered around and hopped from one foot to the other. "How much you pay?"

Ah, or maybe helpful with a price. I eyed him. "One buck."

He waved me away. "No, you leave."

"Two bucks."

His gaze flitted around and settled on me. "Three bucks and you stay."

"Okay, three bucks for both?"

"No, each." He dropped them.

"You're having a laugh, mate. Five bucks, final offer, or we walk." I grabbed Sally's arm, and we turned around.

"Okay, yes."

"Thank you. Drinks?" I held an imaginary glass to my lips and shook it several times towards my mouth. Why do we do that? I mean, if it were a proper drink, I would have just spilt the contents all over me.

"Drinks are for guests, not you."

"How much?"

His eyes darted left and right. "What you want?"

"For now, two beers."

"Five bucks."

"For both?"

"Yes."

"All right, two beers, mate." I hesitated to ask the next question, suspecting how this would play out. But hey ho, in for a peso, in for a Cuban dollar. "Can we buy some food at lunchtime?"

"Food is for guests . . ."

You might think you know the rest.

You'd be wrong.

"No food."

"No food?"

"None."

As the morning progressed, the waves crashed against the beach loudly and without rhythm, as erratic as my thoughts. Any kind word or loving gesture from Sally would make me wonder if I'd got it all wrong, if we could patch things up. Then, she'd be Sally, and I'd sink back into pessimism.

At lunchtime, I went for a walk and found a little bar and a woman keen to engage me in conversation. *Haha*, I thought, *still got the old magic.* This was good to know, given that after the vacation, I might be back on the dating scene. The idea excited me—before I remembered my previous experiences. The thought of all the time and effort involved in meeting and dating new women made me feel as if I were standing at the foot of a tall mountain wondering how on earth I'd ever reach the peak. And I have a fear of heights, remember.

I could only assume the sight of me half-naked in swimming shorts was fuelling the woman's flirting. My illusion was shattered when she dropped her voice and said, "Want to buy a sandwich? Got a friend who makes the best sandwiches, only two bucks each. Want some, do you?" My ego deflated faster than a beach ball stabbed with a knife.

At least the sandwiches, which were handed over conspiratorially in a brown envelope, were excellent.

When we returned to our casa, Sally and I were greeted by Paul. "Hey, my friends, you eat here tonight?"

I turned to Sally. "What do you reckon, Sal?"

She twisted her mouth, and suddenly her eyes lit up. "I fancy lobster and big prawns. I've had a hankering for that since Cienfuegos."

Paul stroked the black-and-white stubble on his chin. "Yeah, no problem for my honoured guests."

"How long?" I asked.

He stared into the distance, moving his head from side to side. "Two hours, max."

I looked at Sally for confirmation. She gave me a thumbs up. "Yeah, we'll have four beers while we wait and eat about eight?"

"Good, yes, I must go." With that, he shuffled into the house and returned a minute later on a bike. Then Sonia, the queen of liars, came out, set up a table in the front garden, and served us four beers.

"All very mysterious," I said.

"Wonder where he's gone off to?" Sally said, taking a sip of beer.

"Probably to exchange his cycle for a bucket of prawns." I glugged back some beer.

Sally giggled and reached across the table to hold my hand. "Our last night here. Let's go wild and go to that bar, Calle something."

Staring into the distance, I considered my options. My fraying nerves were being held together by the thinnest of threads. And I needed a respite from my mind. A bar would be a distraction. And maybe a distraction would help me finally figure out what to do about Sally. "Okay, let's go after dinner."

She squealed and squeezed my hand. I gave her hand a gentle squeeze in return then pulled back my hand.

An hour and a half later, Paul returned without his bike. My eyebrows flew up in surprise. Had I been correct in my assumption? I'd been mostly joking. He cracked a beer and sat down with us, wiping his brow. He smelt of sweat, fish, and the sea—quite a heady combination on a humid evening and after two beers.

I had to ask. "Did you swap your cycle for the food tonight?"

He stared at me, perplexed. Then his eyes widened and brightened. He threw his head back and laughed. "No. I go out on my boat, catch, and bring it back."

My jaw dropped, and I looked at Sally, who appeared equally taken aback by the revelation. "I thought you'd gone round to a mate's and bought some."

"No, I went fishing and caught your dinner."

This touched me. "Thank you. That's very accommodating of you."

"Not at all, you're my guests. I want you to be happy to go home and tell everyone how great the Cuban people are." He gulped his beer.

"Your English is excellent." This had proven to be a good conversation starter, and I was eager to hear more about Paul's life. "How come?"

"I lived in Miami for many years. I picked up the language there."

I took a swig of my beer as well. "Do you still live in America now? Are you back for the holidays?"

"No, I went to make money and now I come back. I tell the authorities I made a terrible mistake and now I am back forever."

"Wow, your entire family went and came back?" I'd learned earlier that he had a wife and children.

"No, just me. My family stayed here. I wanted to give

them a better life, and now I can with the savings from America. Family is everything."

"How sad that you had to go through that." I admired his dedication to his family, though. Guilt invaded my thoughts. I'd moved to London, away from my kids, who lived in North-East England, in pursuit of my love for Dawn—one of many occasions when I considered a relationship to be my one last hope.

I consoled myself with the thought that a couple of weeks after I got back to England, I'd see my sons and parents for our annual Christmas get-together. It was always a time to celebrate. My heart quickly sank again. What would I have to celebrate? During my depressive periods, all I wanted was to cut myself off from everyone, including family. Would I be able to go through with the visit if Sally and I broke up? Another uncertainty to add to the pile.

Our last night in Varadero. Armed with the trusty Lonely Planet guidebook (in the absence of Google, this had become my new God), we set off to Calle 62. At least it was an opportunity to drown my sorrows. My heart just wasn't in the trip anymore. All I wanted was for it to be over, and to get away from Sally.

We arrived to find a veritable street party. The venue heaved with people.

"Oh babe, fire-eaters. And I love this tune! Let's dance." Sally pulled me towards a mass of tangoing locals.

I tugged her back. "Yeah, let's grab a table first."

She relented. "Fabulous idea. Some mojitos too?"

We grabbed a vacant table and I sorted out our cocktails. The atmosphere was fantastic. As we sipped our drinks, I observed the locals dancing—in particular, a young couple who seemed wildly in love. I stared at them with a mixture of admiration and envy. I wanted what they had. Instead, I had Sally, who couldn't even bear to admit to people that we were dating.

I knocked back my drink and ordered two more, still watching the couple. I wondered if they were the Cuban salsa champions. It wouldn't have surprised me. I pointed them out to Sally. "Have you been watching those two? So, in love, and amazing dancers."

"Oh, yeah, they're pretty good." She nodded her head along to the music.

"Good? They're superb. Absolutely fantastic."

"Yeah, so they're brilliant at dancing. So what?"

I put my mouth to her ear. "Look at them. See how in love they are? Why can't we be like that?"

She pulled away. "We love each other. What are you on about, darling?"

"Yeah, you say that," I said, feeling brave in the haze of the alcohol, "but do you love me? How far are you prepared to go to show your feelings for me?"

"I'm here with you now. What's your problem? This is our last night here. Why not enjoy yourself?"

"Yeah, you're right. You're always right. How could I ever doubt you?" My sarcasm didn't appear to register with her.

Several more drinks later, enamoured with the couple and their dancing, I bought them a drink each—her a Cristal and him a Bucanero. I'm not sure what they thought of me as I stumbled towards them, knocking chairs, tables, and ladies out of the way. "I love you guys," I said, slurring my words and pulling them both in for a hug. "You're amazing. Your dancing. I'm jealous of how in love you are. I love you two."

When I stepped back, they stared at me. "Gracias," the woman said. They gawped at each other and shrugged.

Suddenly feeling unwell, I headed back to Sally. "I feel dodgy, baby," I said, holding my stomach.

"Me too." She rubbed her belly.

"Do you think it was the ice in the cocktails?"

"Or that lobster or the prawns tonight, darling."

"Maybe Sonia poisoned us. The treacherous old hag." I still hadn't forgiven her for lying to me, but I knew my reaction was out of proportion. I knew at whom my anger was aimed.

Now, there are two occasions when you should not break wind. The first is when you have headphones on, as it's hard to judge the noise levels. I've found this out the hard way, on public transport. My usual defence is to stare at a nearby passenger with disgust and shake my head and hope other passengers blame the poor innocent person.

The second is when you have a dicky tummy. You might think it's safe, and nine hundred and ninety-nine times out of a thousand it is. As it turned out, on this night, we found ourselves in that one in a thousand situation.

After a voluminous episode of wind there followed an ominous "Oh, oh, oh no, surely not, give me some tissue quick. Wait, I'm going behind that bin." There was a clenched-bum shuffle and then: "Oh dear lord, no, NO."

Now, I'm a gentleman, so I'm too polite to say which one of us it was. But their first name begins with the letter *S* and ends in *ally*. As I disposed of the incriminating evidence, aka the soiled knickers, in said bin, I couldn't help but chuckle to myself. It felt a tiny bit like poetic justice.

20

PROPOSAL

I woke early to make sure we caught our bus to Havana. And also, to sneak a peek at Sally's phone. I knew I'd feel guilty about it, but I needed answers. I needed to read the messages, scour her social media, and find out the truth. No more speculation. But Sally woke up too, thwarting my nefarious plan.

We stumbled and fumbled about. My head boomed, and my belly verged on volcanic. I barely made it to the bathroom in time. As I exited, Sally shoved past me. I soon heard reverberating noises and feared the worse. When Sally finally emerged, she stared at me with sad eyes, holding her stomach for dear life. I returned her stare. And with a simple shake of her head, we had a new plan: back to bed. I intended to stay awake to implement my cunning scheme, but my hangover knocked me out.

When I woke again, daylight was streaming into the room. Nausea hit me as I gingerly sat up. I felt as if I'd passed a hedgehog through my bottom. I squinted in agony as I checked the time on my phone. The booked bus was long gone, and I had no clue what time other buses departed.

Suddenly feeling panicky, I woke Sally, and a frantic quarter of an hour later, we'd showered, changed, packed, and were out the door. On the main road, I tried to flag a taxi. Four of them passed us by, but the next one didn't. I say taxi, but more a motorbike with a two-seater carriage attached. The driver hitched our backpacks to the shelf underneath us and set off in a hurry, seemingly determined to hit every pothole, crack, and crater in the road and disturb the already unsettled contents of our stomachs. At one point Sally heaved but somehow managed to hang on to the contents of her tummy, as well as her dignity.

Halfway to the bus station, the driver brought the vehicle to a shuddering halt. She got out and pulled the bike over to the side of the road.

Thoughts of catastrophe galloped into my head; I scanned the road for alternative transportation. Sally drew her legs towards her chest and emitted the odd groan and whimper. Then I noticed that the driver had gone to a small box on the side of the two-seater carriage. She whipped out a canister and a funnel, unscrewed the petrol cap, inserted the funnel, and tipped the canister into it.

A fuel stop, and we were off again. Perhaps this was normal, but it had struck me as unusual. One of the joys of travelling—I never would have experienced something like that in the UK.

I took a last look around Varadero. It hadn't been quintessentially Cuban in the sense that its vibe was that of a manufactured tourist resort, but it certainly had a history. Distracted by the situation with Sally, I'd missed an opportunity to delve deeper into that history. But I'd enjoyed the conversations I'd had with locals and had learned more about the reality of Cuba for its people. I was glad we'd ventured further than a closeted resort. And I'd enjoyed the beach. It was the best one I'd visited in my entire life. Yes, better even than New Brighton in its heyday.

Then I looked ahead and steeled myself for what was coming next. The trip was drawing to an end, and I couldn't put off a confrontation much longer.

∾

At the coach station, we found a taxi. The driver wanted twenty bucks to take us to Havana, five dollars more than I'd expected, but I was too ill to negotiate and had no desire to take my chances on a coach.

Less than two hours after setting off, we were on the familiar Malecón. Sally poked my shoulder. "Babe, it's too early, not even midday yet. How are we going to check in to our apartment?"

"There's a twenty-four-hour reception."

"You sure?"

I grabbed the paper confirmation of my booking. "Yes, check here."

As the taxi pulled up to our accommodation, my heart sank. The concrete of the apartment block was wearing away and falling off in patches, and we appeared to be in a rundown part of the city; the garden surrounding the apartment buildings was overgrown with weeds and thorns. The reality certainly didn't match the pictures I'd viewed online. I shuddered to think about what we'd find inside.

As we clambered out of the taxi, Sally gawped at the building. "Is this it?"

I gulped. "Yeah, don't judge a book by its cover."

"Looks like a council tower block." She scowled.

To be fair, it did, but I bristled. My first home had been in a council tower block before we'd moved to a council house when I was a toddler. "Don't be a snob. Remember, that's where I come from."

She eyed me. "Yeah, I forget that beneath that middle-class exterior lies a chav."

"We weren't chavs. I had a working-class upbringing. Big difference."

"Well, at least you're not that now, otherwise, I wouldn't be with you."

I had no energy for this right now. "Come on, let's get in."

The twenty-four-hour reception turned out to be a grizzled-looking old man wearing a fedora sat in a rocking chair outside the entrance. I handed him the piece of paper with our booking confirmation. He rose creakily and shuffled inside the building and over to the lift.

"At least the lifts don't smell of wee," I whispered to Sally, as we followed him in. In some of the blocks of flats and maisonettes I'd been in and out of as a kid, the stench of piss had been overwhelming.

The lift groaned and creaked as much as the old man as it rose—enough to make me wonder whether it would finish the journey to our apartment on the fifteenth floor. When the doors opened, we stepped out onto a landing. Seeing the door to our apartment open, I stepped inside to find myself in a spacious hallway, where I was greeted by a middle-aged woman with auburn hair wearing a fixed smile.

She bowed slightly. "Welcome, Mr and Mrs Kelly." I was too tired and ill to correct her. She stepped aside and ushered us through a doorway.

Oh my goodness. The suite was amazing. There was a large living room with an open-plan kitchen, a massive bedroom, and an en-suite bathroom. A concrete balcony, complete with sun loungers, a table, and chairs, wrapped around three sides of the flat. I stepped out. In the distance was the Malecón, and beyond it, the sea. A spectacular view.

You really couldn't judge a book by its cover.

I gazed at Sally, who'd come up beside me, and made a *not bad* face.

She grabbed my arm. "Darling, this is amazing. I love it.

And those views are stunning. You've done well this time." She ruffled my hair. A sense of pride welled up before I caught and suppressed it. I liked my booking; I didn't need validation from her.

Our host stepped outside as well. "Mr Kelly, our cleaner is about to arrive, and we are not yet ready for you. But you can stay if you want. Can I offer you both mojitos?"

"Not for me, thank you."

"Nor me," Sally said.

Refusing cocktails? Goes to show how ill we were. By this stage of the holiday, we'd drunk far more mojitos than water. Normally, though, my hangover would have dissipated by now. Instead, I felt as sick as I had earlier that morning. Maybe I had a tummy bug?

Remembering my manners, I said, "I'm Kevin, this is Sally, and what's your name?"

She smiled, in a more relaxed way this time. "Elsa."

"Well, Elsa, this apartment is amazing. Could we have something non-alcoholic?"

"Of course." She disappeared into the apartment.

I followed suit and plonked myself down in an armchair. Sally sat on the sofa across from the chair. Both were the colour of cream. The luxurious apartment featured clean lines and a neutral palette. Only the pictures, flowers, and ornaments provided splashes of colour, mostly red.

Elsa returned with tonic water infused with freshly squeezed lemon and lime. *My God that hits the spot.* I felt an instant boost.

I drained the glass and turned to her. "Elsa, may I ask you about Cuba and Fidel? I'm interested in knowing more about the country, but not everyone wants to talk."

Sally stood and went out to the balcony.

To my delight, Elsa's face brightened. "What would you like to know?"

"Do you enjoy living here?"

She straightened. "Yes, I am patriotic. I love my country and want the best for Cuba. It's cultured and diverse."

"What about closer ties with America?"

She sat down in the chair to my right. "Despite what you may read or hear, we Cubans want to be close to America. Many of our friends and families live there, and family is important to us." She peered downwards, seemingly collecting her thoughts. "Europe is far away, and the produce we import from there is expensive. It will be better and cheaper for us to do so from America. I want us to be friendly with each other." She took a sip of water then added, "I want to keep our Cuban identity and our way of life—with a focus on family, good health, and education. But with a better standard of living."

I hadn't realised the Cubans relied on Europe for their imports. No wonder food was expensive here. It was shipped nearly halfway around the world. But in my research of Cuba, I had come across information about the country's excellent health and education systems. I leant in. "Are things improving?"

She nodded. "Yes, but slowly. Our leaders are nervous about moving too fast." She waved a finger toward me. "They saw what happened in Europe with the communist countries and the leaders overthrown. They want to keep their power but improve things for the citizens."

I leant further forward. "What do you think about what Fidel did?"

Her brow furrowed. "He was a man of his time. He grew up in a period where you were with the Americans or against them. After he came to power, to keep it, he made friends with the Russians. He focused on foreign affairs to the detriment of the domestic side." She studied my empty glass, which I'd set on the coffee table in front of us, then rose, strode to the kitchen, and returned with a jug of the tonic water.

I thanked her as she refilled my glass. "Were the people scared of him? Did they love or hate him?"

She set down the jug and sat down again. "Hmm, all three. He was our leader for decades, and he was Cuban, so we loved him for that. But life was tough for us. He could have been less aggressive with America."

"So, what about Raúl, his brother? What's he like?"

She pulled her lips together and pondered my question for a moment before nodding quickly. "He is different from Fidel. Yes, he is a communist, but he is keener to fix the economy to improve our standard of living." She waggled her finger. "He is not charismatic like his brother, but so what. He tries his best. But maybe he won't succeed. He is still part of the old guard."

"Who will be the leader after Raúl?"

Her eyes lit up. "There is a young man, Miguel Díaz-Canel. Very charming. One of the new leaders coming through. Perhaps he will be president next."

"Elected?" I asked tentatively.

She laughed then straightened her blouse. "No, we have elections, but they are not the same as in your country. Yes, we have different candidates and parties, but the Communist Party controls all. So, no election, no."

Enjoying Elsa's openness, I didn't want to push her too far, but I pressed on, my curiosity getting the better of me. "I've found some people reluctant to talk about Fidel. Some even hesitate to use his name."

"But of course. There is some fear there, and for many, their position in Cuba and society is dictated by the Communist Party." She held her thumb and forefinger together and then created a small gap between them. "The control here is more subtle—loss of jobs and status rather than arrests and prison camps. They still exist, but less so, I think."

"Are you optimistic?"

Her lips curled downwards. "Not so much optimistic as

hopeful, I think." Then she turned the tables. "So, tell me, you like Cuba?"

I sat back in my seat. "It's been an experience I won't forget." *Not even with extensive therapy.* It had been a memorable trip, possibly for all the wrong reasons, thanks to Sally. On a positive note, I'd had no near-death experiences. The nightmares and flashbacks resulting from this holiday would be traumatic in a different way. "Many of the people we've met have been friendly and lovely," I said. Elsa beamed. "I have less love for your bureaucracy, buses, Wi-Fi, and shops, but they're an experience all the same." Then she frowned, and I chuckled.

I thought about the UK. In Wales and Scotland, people were proud of their countries. This wasn't as much the case in England, despite its incredible culture and diversity, especially in the cities. We Brits rarely talked about our country or expressed pride in it. I wondered why. Perhaps it had to do with our overall stoic nature and distaste for confidence and pride? National pride was often associated with or mistaken for nationalism, right-wing politics, and xenophobia, so politicians tended to steer clear of the issue for fear of stirring up unwanted debates and accusations that impugned their integrity.

After only a couple of weeks in Cuba, I felt certain that the Cubans genuinely loved their country in a way that the Brits didn't. They had national pride and were vocal about it. We either didn't have it or whispered it quietly behind closed doors.

I couldn't help but draw the comparison to myself. When was the last time I'd taken pride in myself and my achievements? When was the last time I'd expressed my love for myself?

I hoped Cuba could find that perfect amount of economic freedom it was looking for—the kind of freedom that would improve the living standards of its people. It couldn't be a good thing that professionals were being lost to the tourist economy. Yet despite its struggles, this small, isolated country had held its own. Perhaps it was time for this small, isolated man to hold his own too. Seemed I had a lot to learn from the Cubans.

While the cleaner worked her magic, Sally and I sat on the balcony and watched the city beneath us in silence. An uncomfortable one. Was the time right to hold my own and confront Sally? Not yet, I quickly decided. I still didn't know how I wanted to state my case. When I'd confronted Dawn, the evidence was incontrovertible. But how long could I maintain my current state without exploding?

When Elsa popped out to tell us our apartment was ready, I breathed a sigh of relief. "Thank you, Elsa, and thank you for our chat before. Where's a good place to go tonight for New Year's Eve?" In the maelstrom, Sally and I hadn't broached the subject of what we would do that evening.

"Hmm, well there is a hotel at the bottom of this road, nearby, or Cathedral Square, but you'd need to book a ticket. The hotel will sell tickets for both." She stared out at the city. "For many people, New Year's Eve is a time for family and staying indoors. So, it's not such a huge celebration here." She looked at us and smiled. "Enjoy your stay and Happy New Year."

"Thanks again, Elsa." I waved at her as she left then faced Sally, who was leaning over the balcony, shielding her eyes from the sun. "How are you feeling? I'm still ropey."

She twisted around. "Not brilliant."

"I might have a nap. Care to join me?"

She studied me for a moment. "Erm, love to, but I think I'm going to pop down to that Hotel, find out about tonight. There or that Cathedral Square."

"I'll come with you." My desire to keep an eye on her trumped my desire for rest and recuperation.

"No, you take it easy, babes. You look tired. I'll be fine." She caressed my face. "Please, stay."

She wanted to be alone, which was very unlike her.

After she'd left, I lay in bed, my mind racing. She was up to something. There was no way I'd be able to sleep now. I jumped out of bed and immediately regretted it when I dry-heaved. I exhaled slowly a few times to settle myself and my stomach down.

As I made my way to the hotel, the humid air clung to my skin. I could feel it dragging the sweat—and hopefully the toxins—out of my pores. Fifteen minutes later, I arrived at the entrance and walked in hesitantly, hoping to spot Sally before she spotted me.

At the information desk, I found some marketing material about a grand gala evening at the hotel. To the right were tables and chairs, all filled with people on their phones. That had to be the Wi-Fi hot spot. Aha, there she was. Sally had her back to me and was talking to the screen. I edged a little closer until I could hear snippets of the conversation.

". . . lonely . . . safe . . . beach . . . bongo . . . miss . . ."

I could hear a man's voice. Certainly not Harry's squeaky dulcet tones. My heart raced, my palms sweated, and my nose blocked up. My bladder was also ready to burst, but that could wait. I took several deliberate breaths as I edged even closer. Now I could hear Sally clearly.

"I can't wait to see you when I get back. I've missed you so much, and I promise this is the last time I'll go away on my own. Next Christmas it'll be me and you. Tell me what present you bought me—I don't like surprises."

The man said something, and Sally squealed in delight. I

thought about jumping forward and confronting her there and then, but fear gripped me. Instead, I edged backwards, towards the information desk. I tried to stay out of sight but close enough to spy.

"Excuse me, sir, can I help you?" said a woman behind the desk. When I didn't answer, she persisted. "Hello? Do you need help?"

I turned to the receptionist, who stared at me. "Oh, hi, yeah, erm, just looking . . . at your gala evening tonight." I peeped over at Sally.

"Would you like tickets?"

I faced the woman and cleared my throat. "Yes, why I'm here, to buy gala tickets for tonight. Two, please."

As I picked up the tickets off the desk and thanked the receptionist, a voice behind me made me jump.

"Hey, what are you doing out of bed? Hope you've not been spying on me?"

I laughed nervously. "No, I, erm, couldn't sleep and I spotted the advert for the gala evening, so I've bought us two tickets." I waved them at her and forced a grin. "So yeah, that's what we'll be doing later. New Year's Eve here at this prestigious hotel. Exciting, hey?"

"Yes, if you say so." She cocked her head. "Are you okay? Your skin looks kind of grey."

I smiled, exposing my crooked teeth. "I'm fine, marvellous, still ill but almost better."

"Well, come and sit down. Some Wi-Fi here." She ushered me to follow her.

"Excellent," I said, rubbing my hands together. "You talk to anyone? Back home? Chat to anyone?"

"Just spoke to Harry." She half-turned away and rubbed her mouth.

A blatant lie. I managed to ask, "And how is the little monkey?"

We sat down. "Don't call him that. He hates that nickname. He's good. Everybody's fine."

"Great. Marvellous. Super. That's bloody brilliant."

Sally eyed me doubtfully. "You okay?"

"Sorry, a bit overexcited. New Year's Eve and all that."

I was most certainly not okay. Who was the mystery man? John? Had to be. My stomach twisted, turned itself inside out, and then flung itself back to normal, leaving me nauseous and disorientated.

At the gala that evening, we sat at a table of strangers. And as I looked at Sally, I felt as if she were the biggest stranger of all. I kept replaying the afternoon's events. Had I heard right? Had it been John's voice? I might have misunderstood. The only thing helping me keep it together was the belief that I still needed more evidence. More proof.

I'd messaged Sean and Paddy that afternoon.

I'm sorry for being such a dick after that meditation. Messed up big time and I need your help. Can't go into details, but can you check Sally's Facebook page, see what she's posted while here and if there are any posts, pictures, or videos of me? Anything. I'll explain all when I'm back.

Both agreed I'd been an enormous dick and then asked how I was. I lied and told them I was fine. I wasn't.

"You've been quiet tonight, darling."

I jerked out of my thoughts and half-smiled at Sally. "Yeah, still feeling rough." I took a sip of my red wine. It was a shame I was too sick and preoccupied to enjoy it, as it was exquisite.

I looked around. The clientele seemed to be mostly tourists and a sprinkling of locals—richer ones. Perhaps they were apparatchik, or maybe businesspeople starting to benefit from the liberalisation unfolding in the country.

"Look at us," Sally said with a grin, "ringing in the new year in Havana. Who would have believed it?"

"Yeah, I know. I wonder where we'll be this time next year." I sat on my hands to avoid chewing my nails.

She straightened and stared at me. "Well, by then I expect you will have proposed to me."

If I'd had wine in my mouth, I would have choked on it. Had I misread everything? I cleared my throat. "Husband number four, hey?"

"If you play your cards right, darling." She winked at me.

One hand escaped, so I clasped my wineglass to provide it with something to do. "So where will this proposal take place?"

She brushed her hair upwards dramatically. "Hmm, exotic, abroad . . . Taj Mahal, maybe? And I want an antique platinum ring with a massive sparkly diamond."

"India?" I blew air out of my mouth. "Not sure about that. Ring sounds expensive too."

"Don't be crass and talk about money," she snapped. "But the going rate is three times your monthly take-home pay." She tapped her ring finger and looked at me pointedly.

I stared at her. "Where did you get that from?"

"Read it in a magazine. Anyway, I kept my other engagement and wedding rings. They're for my retirement. Number three wanted his back, the cheapskate. Don't end up like that arsehole."

My head was a mess. Why on earth were we talking about marriage, after everything I'd learned over the holiday? What about the flirting, the Rave in the Cave, the text messages, the call . . . ?

"I won't," I muttered, nibbling on some pork and nothing else. I felt worse than I had earlier. "Can we leave after we finish eating? I still feel rotten. What about you?"

She clutched her belly. "Not great."

As we were leaving, well before midnight, I remembered

the texts I'd sent to Sean and Paddy. Proof. I needed proof if it killed me. I grabbed Sally's hand. "Can we sit down for a bit before we hike up the hill back to the apartment? I want to send a message to my family for New Year's Eve. Won't take long."

"I don't mind." She whipped out her phone.

I'd figured she wouldn't.

We took a seat near the reception desk, and it wasn't long before a few messages popped up. I saw a couple each from Sean and Paddy. I tackled them after sorting out my New Year's Eve messages to my family.

From Sean:

Loads of posts, pictures, and videos but none of you, you don't get a mention at all.

In one post, it says something about being there on her own.

From Paddy:

Some video of her in a pink Cadillac, but not seen anything about you.

Strange but in her profile, it says she's single. What's going on, mate? We're worried about you.

My heart sank, but it still wasn't enough to confront her with. The relationship status might have been a hangover from when we split up. Or was I being naïve? I went to the toilet, and when I came back into the reception area, I saw Sally had my phone in her hand. Rage swelled. How dare she read my messages? Yet, this could work in my favour.

She sees the messages I've sent, confronts me, then I can confront her with it all.

My anger subsided. Now I hoped she'd read my messages. I pretended not to see, and when I got back to her, my phone was on the table.

But I got no reaction. She'd left the ball firmly in my court.

We walked back to the apartment; our silence matched by

that of the city. Elsa had been right—New Year's Eve was a quiet affair here.

I got up shortly before midnight. I couldn't sleep; my head refused to let matters lie. Plus, I always stayed up for midnight on New Year's Eve, even when I was on my own. Out on the balcony, I shivered in the evening's cool. Below, I could hear the occasional sounds coming from family gatherings, and when midnight arrived, a distant solitary cannon fired twelve battery rounds. Two local dogs joined in the noise to bark in the new year.

A new year. What would it bring me? An engagement with Sally? Unlikely. Sex without Viagra? Even less likely. What I wanted more than anything was peace of mind. To live without the stress, anxiety, and depression that had defined the previous year. I needed to find a way to push through to the other side of those emotions.

I wandered back into the bedroom, where Sally still slept soundly. In the kitchen, I poured myself a glass of water and sipped on it. Its coldness gave me the chills—that and the argument, both philosophical and moralistic, that raged in my weary head.

There were strong and passionate arguments about both the rightness and wrongness of what I was about to do: invoke the nuclear option. I clutched the side of my head and gingerly shook it, increasing the pace until the pain forced me to slow down. My stomach churned.

I stood frozen but shaking, rooted to the spot, taking little sips of water every second or so. When the glass was empty, I put it down, padded into the bedroom, picked up Sally's phone from the nightstand on her side of the bed, and headed to the balcony, where I settled myself on a chair facing the doorway.

I tapped in the passcode—Harry's birthday—and the mobile lit up. It was a lucky guess. I was in. No turning back now. The deed was done. Ten minutes later, I had answers to the questions that had been gnawing at me for the whole trip, and long before. And in that certainty, I felt strangely calm.

21

GUT TRUST

I'd always hated the last day of a holiday. This one stirred up many emotions for me, a veritable mix of them. I knew what action I wanted to take with Sally now. The only issue was the timing.

The first order of the day was to head back to the hotel down the road, as Sally needed her Wi-Fi fix and I wanted to check on our flight details. In the busy reception area, we squeezed into a table for four with two older ladies. The internet was temperamental. There were many comparisons I could make to it. "How's your signal?" I asked Sally.

"Fine." She didn't look up. A swipe here, a tippity-tap there.

"Mine keeps cutting out. I might need to swap seats with you at some point." *Like now.*

She held up a palm. "Yeah, I'm in the middle of something. In a minute."

I didn't bother hiding my annoyance. "I could do with getting online to check our flights and make sure there are no emails I need to see."

"As I said, doing something, won't be long." Her palm became a finger. The corner of her mouth had curled up.

"Yeah, it's just if our flight has changed, I need to find out now, to make sure we travel to the airport on time."

Her head snapped up. "Stop hassling me. I said give me a moment. You're very stressed today. What's up with you?"

What was up with me? I could have laughed. I hadn't been this depressed since, well, Dawn. I'd never wanted to be in this position again, had vowed I'd never be that man again. Yet here I was, several years later, the same man, making the same mistakes, on the path to having another nervous breakdown. The nervous breakdown part didn't scare me. The aftermath did. The long, hard slog, the endless days and nights of feeling my life wasn't worth living, the descent into self-medicating to numb the pain.

I'd thought we loved each other, that Sally was the real deal, my happily ever after. But how could she be when I'd stooped to going through her phone to find evidence of her unfaithfulness?

I'd hoped going through her mobile would satisfy my desire for answers. But this morning, all the calm I'd felt the previous night was gone. The urge to grab her phone again, to spy more, grew. I wanted to do this more than anything. This wasn't normal behaviour. This wasn't love.

Sally stood. "Right, now you can sit here."

"What? Oh, yeah, thank you." I got out of my seat and moved around the backs of the chairs while Sally shuffled over. *Come on, hurry.* Sitting down, I rejoiced—I had a signal. No changes to our flight and nothing pressing in my inbox. There were some more messages from Sean and Paddy, but I possessed no energy or desire to open them up. I ignored them.

"You finished? Like to send a message to Harry."

"I thought you were . . . erm, doesn't matter." Harry? Or someone else? Who was she texting? I stamped down the questions. I needed to stop feeding the beast of obsession.

I got up and moved around the back of the chairs again as

Sally shimmied to her original seat. The hotel guests must have thought we were playing musical chairs. No one seemed keen to join.

Done with my phone, I smiled at the women across from me, and they returned the gesture. "Hi, I'm Kevin, this is Sally. Where are you ladies from?"

"Louisiana," one of the women drawled. "I'm Hilda, and this is my best friend Dorothy."

They explained that they were on an "educational tour". It was the only way they, as Americans, were allowed to travel to Cuba. Though they'd intended to go on all the organised trips, the "rebellious spirit of Cuba" had corrupted them, and they were doing their own thing. I suspected they were rebellious before they got to Cuba. They didn't seem to care what anybody thought of them. I wished I had that about me.

"Right," Sally said, finally finished. "Let's head back. I need to pack, and I want to chill on the balcony for a bit."

As soon as we'd left the hotel, I stopped. I needed to clear my head, away from Sally. I needed to think. "Sal, I'm going to go for a walk. Still not feeling my best, to be honest. The fresh air will do me good."

"Okay, I'll meet you back at the apartment."

While I waited at a set of traffic lights, a Cuban teenager appeared at my side. "Hi, my friend, how are you?"

I peered around, momentarily confused. Was he talking to me? "Yeah, great, thank you, and you?"

"Today is a special day for us Cubans," he said with a grin. "The anniversary of the glorious revolution."

I smiled. "Great. Happy revolution day."

"Thank you. Where are you from, my friend?"

"Live in London now but originally from the Wirral, near Liverpool." An alert in my belly was sounding off. Something didn't feel right. I looked at the traffic light, willing it to go green.

He edged closer. "Liverpool? Oh, I love The Beatles and football. Who do you support?"

"Erm, yeah, Everton is my team."

"I love Everton! They're a great team."

I softened. What a lovely young man, friendly and chatty. I ignored my body; probably nothing. Just my illness and state of mind. "They used to be. Not so much nowadays. What do you do in Havana?"

"I am a student. One day, I will become a famous Cuban engineer."

The light turned green. "Brilliant, I hope that works out for you. You have a great day." I stepped into the road.

"Oh, my friend, before you go. I am off to visit my grandma and she has no milk—can you spare a buck or two? She lives on her own and only has me to care for her."

I knew it. Such a shame. Why hadn't I listened to my gut?

I handed the boy two bucks. Even though I didn't believe his story, I wanted to teach myself a lesson. Plus, I had some cash left that I wouldn't be able to exchange or spend back home.

As I walked, I took a deep breath and tried to feel into my body. What was it telling me to do about Sally? I needed to listen.

For the next hour or so, I wandered along the Malecón. I came across the reopened US embassy. Previously occupied by the Swiss, it had been considered a US interest in Cuba until 2015. Outside the building, one solitary US flag was surrounded by Cuban flags. I'd read about staff in the embassy projecting anti-government messages outside their offices. The Cuban solution: to surround the offending messages with Cuban flags. I loved this. If only all disputes in the world could be resolved through a flag fight. If so, I mused, would Morris dancers and their little hanky flags rule the world?

I wondered briefly if I could resolve my situation with

Sally through flags but couldn't think of any way that would work. Our situation required communication. The thought of that filled me with fresh dread.

To get back to our casa from the embassy, I needed to cross a busy six-lane road with cars travelling in both directions. I stared across the road, rooted to the spot, scared witless. My breathing quickened and became shallow. My heart sped along. Then I spotted a gap and, without another thought, ran through, looking left and right and back again and back the other way until I reached the other side.

I bent over double. I'd done it. Even though it was the last thing on earth I'd wanted to do. I knew I could be brave when I wanted to. At that moment, I resolved that when I returned to the apartment, I would talk to Sally. No waiting around. No messing about. Time to confront her about John. About everything. I would listen to my gut.

"Have you got something you want to say?" Sally asked. Shuffling my feet, I stared down at them, trying to summon the exhilaration I'd felt running across the road. "Well, come on, our taxi will be here soon."

I rubbed my fingers and thumbs together. "Yeah . . . Yeah . . . I just wanted to say . . . Well . . . on this holiday . . . you know . . . me and you . . ."

She folded her arms. "Come on, spit it out."

"Well . . . yes, I . . ." I bottled it. "I'm sad we're going home." I just couldn't bear the thought of being sat next to each other on the plane after having the conversation I wanted to have with her.

She shook her head. "Yeah, me too. Now hurry. We need to be downstairs in five minutes."

At the airport, I bid a silent goodbye to the Benny Hill uniforms, and Cuba. The trip had certainly been enlightening.

The Cubans I'd spoken to loved and believed in their country in a way that had forced me to think about my lack of love for and belief in myself. Despite my current anguish, I was grateful.

Yes, the customer service was, overall, the worst I'd ever experienced in my life, but when I'd needed compassion and kindness, I'd received it. I hoped the Cubans would keep hold of the great things in their country as they navigate their future.

While the situation with Sally had soured huge parts of the trip, I'd rediscovered my love of travel and been reminded of the importance of taking calculated risks, escaping my everyday life, and experiencing new cultures. Sadness washed over me as I wondered whether I'd ever be able to travel again if I was single. Maybe I could finally travel on my own? I shuddered. One step at a time.

On the flight home, on a plane that looked as if it had been modern in the seventies, with food seemingly leftover from that decade too—I now understood why the tickets had been so cheap—I lapsed into thoughts of Dawn.

I'd been sitting at my dining table in my flat, my hands shaking.

I put my phone on the table and stared at the screen, at the picture of Dawn, taken on New Year's Eve, dancing with her sister, the rest of her family, and a man. I recognised the man.

She'd told me she was too ill to come to mine on New Year's, said she'd contracted laryngitis. I'd been gutted. It was the umpteenth time that we'd not be together for a significant event. There were always plausible reasons—some illness or catastrophe or family crisis—but each time they came, I accepted them with less patience and understanding.

That New Year's Eve had been the last straw. I'd sat for days afterwards piecing the puzzle together with a sense in my belly that something was off.

The photos were on Facebook, on her sister's page. Dawn had told me she'd deleted her account because of her mental health. I understood that. Social media was the last place I wanted to be when I was depressed or anxious. But I'd just created a fake profile and found her.

I logged out and back in, under my proper account. No Dawn. Only one explanation: she was still on Facebook and had blocked me. But why?

The clawing anxiety in the pit of my stomach scratched its way up into my chest. My hands continued shaking. I had no control over them. I inspected the photos again. Dawn dancing with that man. They looked as if they were a couple —but how could they be, after what she'd said to me?

She picked up as soon as I called.

"Hi, baby, how are you?"

"You've blocked me on Facebook," I blurted, despite my dry mouth. "Why?"

"Babe, no, I'd never block you, don't be silly now. Remember, I deleted my account for my mental health. Can't deal with this now. I'm ill and this is how you treat me?"

"I know you've blocked me on Facebook. I've seen your profile."

"I'm hanging up."

"I also spotted the photos from New Year's Eve—of you and him."

There was silence on the other end, and then a couple of sniffles.

"Baby, I never wanted to hurt you. I never meant for any of this. I'm sorry. I need to go." The line went dead. Moments later, my mobile pinged, notifying me of a message.

I can't do this right now. Sorry. Never meant to hurt you. Love you. Can we meet up next week?

My shaking hand managed to type out a reply.

You said you were divorced. You said you lived with your son on your own. But you're still married, aren't you? That was your husband in the pictures.

I'm sorry. We are. But I don't love him. I only love you. We're married in name only. Please don't leave me. I need you. I can't bear the thought of losing you.

I can't do this anymore, I replied. *The pain is unbearable. You were the love of my life. I thought we would grow old together. Take care.*

Please meet me. I'll explain everything. You said you'd never give up on me. Yet here you are. Giving up on me. Don't do this.

I put the phone down and walked away. How was I in this situation? How could I have been so ignorant of what was going on, right in front of me? Why was I so blinded by love?

I slumped face down on my bed and screamed into the pillow. When the screams subsided, the tears came.

I will never, ever put myself in this situation again, I vowed.

22

DING, DING, SECONDS OUT, ROUND 22

Roger stopped the car outside Sally's. I helped him unload it. He carried Sally's bags; I cast aside mine at the end of the drive.

At the bottom of the steps leading to her front door, Sally turned to face me. "Well, that was interesting. I'm tired." Her eyes flitted to Roger, who stood next to her.

"Yeah. It certainly was." Thoughts flickered through my head. *Should I, or shouldn't I?* My stomach twisted and turned. *If not now, then when?*

"Right, okay, well as I said . . ." She stared at me, clearly waiting for me to leave. Her eyes darted to Roger again. "Roger, can you take my bags in?" She tilted her head towards the front door.

It took a few moments for Roger's alcohol-addled brain to kick in. "Oh yes, of course, babes. I'll open up." He fumbled with the keys and opened the door then went inside with her backpack.

Sally pulled me aside. "So, yeah, thank you, darling, for a lovely time away. Was the best. You're the greatest."

She moved forward to kiss me. I took a step back and held my palms out. "Interesting."

She shook her head. "Sorry, you've lost me. What?"

"How you waited for Roger to be out of earshot before thanking me and telling me I'm the best. Why's that?"

Sally's eyes darted from left to right. She turned and checked the front door. "I . . . I . . . I . . . don't know what you mean."

"Almost as if you didn't want him to hear you say that to me. Why's that?"

Looking nervous, she fiddled with her hair. "I don't know what's going on here, but you're being weird and paranoid, and I haven't got time for this." She turned.

I stepped forward. "Single beds, thank God."

She swivelled round. "What?" Her voice had risen an octave.

I stared directly at her. "Lots of things I heard and noticed. I only just put it all together on New Year's Eve, though. The night before we flew to Cuba, you said to Roger, 'Single beds, thank God'." My heart rate crept up, but I maintained my stare. "Then there was that message to him. You said, 'It's been a nightmare. I'm scared and wish I were home, sharing a bottle of wine with you.'"

"Oh, don't be ridiculous, Kevin," she sputtered, waving her arms around. "You think Roger and I are an item? Do you realise how stupid you sound?"

I took a step forward. "Oh, I'm certain you're not together. I know this because you portrayed the trip with me to be hellish, yet you just told me I'm the best. You're a liar," I said evenly.

"That's it!" she squeaked. "I've had enough!" She whirled around and walked away.

I followed her to her steps. "What I ever saw in him I'll never understand."

Sally turned immediately. This time, anger flashed across her face. "Have you been going through my phone, reading my texts?"

"That one I noticed over your shoulder. I thought you were talking about someone else, that John. Do you remember him? The one you were seeing when we first started dating?"

"I can't believe you read my messages," she spluttered. "Outrageous."

"What, like you did on New Year's Eve? You didn't think I noticed you, but I did. Why would you check my phone? I've never been unfaithful to you. Never given you a reason to doubt me."

"I . . . I . . ." She cupped her mouth with her hand.

I turned to walk away then turned around again, a dramatic gesture that allowed me several seconds to gather my thoughts and return to sparring with her. "You told me you'd stopped seeing John after our Margate trip."

"I did," she said, looking at me pleadingly. "Not seen him since."

This time, I couldn't contain the anger. "Liar!" I said, thrusting my finger at her. I took a deep breath to find a level of control again.

She reached out to touch my arm, but I moved to the side. "Babe," she said, looking everywhere but my face. "I'm not, I promise you."

My eyes narrowed. "So, who were you on the video chat to at the hotel?"

"I don't know what you mean." She glanced at her front door again.

"I saw you, Sally, talking on your phone. And you said 'John' several times." This was a gamble on my part, to press my advantage in the conversation. I hadn't actually heard her say his name. "You told him you loved him and missed him."

"Wh . . . wha . . . what?" She rocked her head.

"Yeah, you thought I didn't see you, but I did." I grimaced. "And for your information, I did read through your messages. I found thousands of them to and from John, dating back to when we first started going out together."

Her mouth dropped, and for a moment, it seemed she couldn't speak. Finally: "I think it's best we just be friends. We're not working out."

My glower widened until it encompassed my entire face. "Not going to happen. We're done. Totally, utterly, and completely over. I never want to see you again."

Before I could fully turn around, she stepped towards me. "But we can still be mates."

I rounded on her. "Why would I want to have anything to do with someone I don't trust and who betrayed me like this? I loved you, and you broke my heart." I thumped my chest. "You knew I'd been cheated on before and how much that hurt me. Yet here you are, doing the same to me. Why?" My voice wobbled as the rush of adrenaline left my body. Suddenly, grief threatened to engulf me.

It was the crack in my armour she needed. Her face hardened, and she sneered at me. "Oh, I think that's a question for you, Kevin. Must be something wrong with you, that the women in your life betray you. Stop feeling sorry for yourself. Shit happens. Now go."

I gazed at her. Her comments hurt yet also softened the blow. I'd worried that she'd deny it all. But I'd got as close to an admission of guilt as I'd likely ever receive from her. My nerves began to settle as relief momentarily worked its way through me. I hadn't been paranoid. I'd been right to confront her.

"Don't make me say it twice."

"I'm going. I'M GOING!" I grabbed my bag and stormed to my car.

In the front seat, I gave myself a pep talk. *I will not cry. I will not get upset.* Big, blobby tears fell from my eyes into my lap. It was all over. I'd never see her again. How would I cope? What would I do? I breathed deeply, found an old tissue in the cupholder, and wiped my tears with a clean corner. I turned the key in the ignition. Nothing. Tried again. Zilch.

"PIECE OF JUNK CAR." I slammed my hands on the steering wheel. The battery was still dead. Not been fixed. I phoned roadside help and then waited, growing increasingly desperate to be in my own home, to let my emotions explode. Closing my eyes, I tried unsuccessfully to concentrate on my breathing, which was shallow and erratic.

Thirty minutes passed.

I spotted Sally's front door open. She poked her head out and glared at me. "Are you stalking me? Leave. Go. NOW."

I wound down the window. "I . . . I can't. My car's dead. I'm waiting for a recovery van."

"Oh, this is typical of you." She slammed the door.

Minutes later, Roger left. He stared at me as he got into his car, seemingly trying to look as threatening as he could, which was about as much so as a kitten. I scoffed. The day just got better and better. And then, just as roadside help arrived, a BMW convertible pulled into Sally's drive. Was that . . .?

No, it couldn't be.

It bloody was.

John.

Despite my despair, I felt sorry for him. Poor bloke didn't know what he was dealing with. Or maybe he did. Either way, he was welcome to Sally. I couldn't wait to drive away and put as much distance as possible between us.

Maybe, just maybe, I'd turned a corner.

23

AFTERMATH

I stared at the attractive woman behind the counter as she repeated what I'd just told her. "Five fish, three large, two small, three large chips, two gravy, and two curry sauce. Anything else?"

"No, that's everything thank you." I smiled, practising my flirting skills.

She glanced at me. "Next?"

They still needed a hell of a lot more work.

"You ordered?" Mum said, meeting me outside the shop.

"Yeah, waiting."

"Paid?"

"Yes, all sorted."

"We said we'd pay. We always buy fish and chips. Here." Mum held out a twenty-pound note. I sighed, knowing this wasn't an argument I'd win. And I couldn't help feeling grateful that for once, my role was to be loved and cared for.

A couple of weeks had passed since Sally and I ended things, and this Christmas get-together at my parents' home, on the Wirral, was a welcome distraction. Fish and chips were a tradition on the first night together, along with the exchanging of gifts.

"Okay," I said, taking the money. "Thank you."

Back at the house, we set the table. My dad had prepared tea and cold drinks.

"You sit down, son," my mum said, urging me toward the dining table.

"Oh, before I forget," I said, still standing. "I have a present for you, Dad—and you too, guys." I smiled at my sons, who'd just walked into the room.

"What is it?" J asked.

"Patience, my young Padawan." I reached into a plastic bag, pulled out the box of cigars, and placed it in the middle of the table. "Here you go, you three."

"Cigars?" D asked.

"Yep. From Cuba. Got them from an official shop, so these are the proper ones."

"Arr," J said with a grin. "You're getting us to smoke. That's naughty."

"Well, you are both over sixteen now." I wagged a finger. "But I'm not encouraging you to smoke. These are genuine Cuban cigars—a treat to be enjoyed."

"Thanks." J leant down and hugged me. I almost burst into tears. Hugs and loving words had the potential to set me off crying these days. They reminded me of what was missing in my life.

"Thank you, FATHER," D said, his deep voice booming as he hugged me. I was always tickled by this tiny idiosyncrasy of his, the way he emphasised the word *father*. Adorable.

I bent a little to hug my dad as he thanked me as well. "I should probably tell you," I said to him. "These cigars are the Winston Churchill ones."

"What?" Disgust filled my father's face. "That Tory bastard —I'll not be touching it," he said, half-serious, his eyes glinting with revulsion. He had unflinching views when it came to politics. Once, he brought home a copy of Mao's famous Little Red Book. A present from his militant union at the time. He'd loved Cuba, with its left-wing politics and communist government. Before becoming a docker, he'd travelled the world as part of a merchant navy for a period, after being in the army. I wondered whether I got some of my wanderlust from him.

"Who said that bastard's name?" my mum said. "No Tories in this house."

"Dot," my dad said, giving her a look and nodding to my sons. "Language."

"They're alright. I'm sure they've heard worse."

"We have!" J and D said in unison.

D turned to me. "Did J tell you about our FIFA game?"

"Shut the flip up, D. No one's listening."

"I am," I said with a grin. "What happened?"

"I beat him eight to two." He laughed.

"Well done, D, I'm proud of you."

"Tea is served," Mum announced.

"You mean dinner, don't you?" I said.

"No, Dad, you soft southerner," J said. "It's tea."

"You tell him, J," my dad said, messing his hair. "Your dad thinks he's in London." He gave me a look. "Well, you're not. You're in the north now."

"Erm, Grandad, Wallasey and Liverpool aren't really in the north. This is like the Midlands."

I sat back in my chair, watching the scene unfold. Amongst my family, my troubles seemed very far away, and it was easy to put on a good show. I knew it would be a totally different story when I returned to my flat once again.

After the showdown with Sally, I'd dumped my bags, tossed my unopened letters on the coffee table, and thrown myself headfirst onto my bed and sobbed for what seemed like hours.

"Mum, do you need a hand?"

"No, you relax. You must be knackered after all that travelling. You can tell us about Cuba."

"Okay, if you insist. I could get used to this." In the background, the television was on, and I laughed when I saw it was *The Benny Hill Show*. "Well, for starters, the immigration control area was like a Benny Hill sketch—women with short skirts being chased by moustached uniformed men."

"Did you meet what's-his-name?" D asked.

"Fidel?" Dad said.

"No," I said, lowering my voice conspiratorially. "He hides in the woods to stop the Americans from trying to assassinate him. And the people won't call him by his name."

"Yeah right," J said.

"No, it's true, and if you say his name out loud, the locals cross themselves."

"Now you're winding us up."

"I'm not. All happened, I tell you." I grinned.

"I saw your posts on Facebook this week about your trip," Mum said. "Hilarious, son. Someone said you should write a book about it all."

I shuddered. Write a book? Me? Where would I even start? Writing books was for narcissists. Anyway, my posts about the trip, I'd written since my return, hadn't and wouldn't touch on the real story, brewing throughout it. I took out my phone. "Could you take a picture of us four with our cigars?"

"Oh, that would be a lovely one, son."

"No cigars," Dad said. "It's a tory one."

"Don't be a dick, Dad."

"I try, but it's not that easy." Like father, like son.

Once we were all sat on the couch with the cigars in our mouths, Mum said, "Say cheese." We all beamed and tried to keep the cigars from falling out of our mouths.

I felt a rush of gratitude for my family. My relationships with them and with myself were the ones that mattered, and I made a new vow: to focus on them.

"So, what happened to Sally?" Mum asked.

"How long have you got? Perhaps I'll write about it in my book, and you can read about it." I winked at her.

"Mummy's little soldier." She roughed my hair.

"I'm not a baby anymore."

"You'll always be mine."

Before putting my phone away, I checked to see if I had any messages. Nothing. I opened up my email and scanned the unsent message to Sally one more time. My finger hovered over the send button. My heart thumped and my breathing quickened.

Breaking up had been the easy part. Staying broken up would require all my determination and resolve. Many minutes and hours lay ahead. It would be a long road. My mind would play tricks on me, tell me I needed to get back together with her. But I knew deep down, in my heart, I needed to stay away from Sally, and relationships with women in general. I couldn't—wouldn't—go through that heartbreak again.

But how would I cope with being on my own? Would I survive without a relationship? Could I have a travel adventure alone?

And what would I do with all the Viagra I had left?

Continued in Book 2 - Midlife Misadventures in Prague

KEVIN KELLY'S ADVENTURE CONTINUES IN MIDLIFE MISADVENTURES IN PRAGUE. READ ON FOR A SUMMARY OF WHAT HAPPENS NEXT...

You can pre-order/buy Midlife Misadventures in Prague, the next book in the series and see what happened next in Kevin Kelly's life. Had Kevin escaped the clutches of Sally? Would he relax into his new single life? Would the braver Kevin last? What happened to all that Viagra?

Available at Amazon - https://books2read.com/Read-Prague

His life is falling apart. Will a weekend away solve his problems or tip him over the edge?

London, England. Kevin Kelly is desperate to forget all about his last relationship. Depressed by his life and failed relations, he convinces himself a Christmas jaunt abroad will fix all his problems. So, he jets off to Prague, with Lesley on a mission of self-preservation.

Unable to forget his past, they suffer a string of disastrous mishaps that threaten their friendship and tips him closer to the edge. But just when Kevin finally believes things are improving, he receives messages from his past that threaten to derail his future.

Can his and Lesley's friendship survive a weekend away as Kevin discovers the truth to happiness?

Written as both a travel book and a trek to self-realisation, this intriguing tale takes you on an extraordinary journey of getting over lost love and heartbreak that will make you cry and laugh out loud. Set among the backdrop of the historic city of Prague, Kevin shares a spirited and humorous ride toward his enlightenment.

Midlife Misadventures in Prague is the second book in the poignant Midlife Misadventures series. If you like raw emotional expeditions, light and dark humour, and excursions abroad, then you'll adore Kevin Kelly's engaging story.

Buy Midlife Misadventures in Prague to roam the world for meaning today!

You can buy Midlife Misadventures in Prague at Amazon

GET THE PREQUEL BOOK AND A BONUS BOOK WITH EXCLUSIVE MATERIALS FOR FREE

Well done, you made it right to the end. You're an awesome human being. Building a relationship with my readers is the best thing about writing.

Join my VIP Readers Club for information on new books and deals, plus a free copy of the exclusive, prequel book to the Midlife Misadventures series, Midlife Misadventures in Margate. Find out what happened before Cuba.

Just visit www.kevinjdkelly.com/landing, click on the free book, and receive this and another FREE bonus book, packed full of extras including pictures, interview with the author and deleted scenes, plus a behind the scenes look at a chapter from the book.

You can buy paperback and hardback versions of this book on Amazon, https://books2read.com/margatepaperback Don't you love the feel and smell of an actual book?

If you want your Book and Bonus materials, get them all for free by signing up here.

ENJOY THIS BOOK? YOU CAN MAKE A DIFFERENCE

Reviews are the most powerful tools in my arsenal. Look at me being all militaristic, but seriously, they help get attention for my books, and the feedback also helps me develop my writing skills.

That's where you come in. Yes, you! The reader.

Honest reviews of my books help bring them to the attention of other readers. If you enjoyed this book, I would be grateful if you could spend just a minute to rate it and write a review (it can be as short as you like).

Thank you very much. Use the links below to jump straight to the Amazon review page:

Amazon US

Amazon UK

COMPETITION AND FREE BONUS BOOK

Enter the competition by clicking the link below:
Yes I want the chance to win a FREE book
By clicking the link you'll be entered into a competition, with the chance to win a signed Hardback or Paperback of Midlife Misadventures in Cuba, or a signed Hardback or Paperback of Midlife Misadventures in Margate.

Act soon as the competition closes, 4 July 2021.

Get your FREE BONUS Book by clicking the link below:
Get my FREE BONUS Book

The bonus book is packed with features including, pictures, author interview, deleted scenes and a before and after look at the first chapter.

Hurry as the bonus book is only available to 4 July 2021.

Copyright © 2021 by Kevin Kelly

All rights reserved.

No part of this book may be reproduced in any form or by any electronic or mechanical means, including information storage and retrieval systems, without written permission from the author, except for the use of brief quotations in a book review.

DISCLAIMER

I value my life and crooked smile—that's why I've changed the names of everyone in this book except mine. Oh, and Mum and Dad. They're called Mum and Dad. Together, they created me and my crooked smile, so I know they value both.

Some characters are an amalgamation of more than one person, and I've taken the liberty to change, invent, and alter specific dates, people, places, events, and details for literary effect.

You should not consider this book anything other than a work of fiction. I have a vivid imagination but a terrible memory.

ACKNOWLEDGMENTS

A huge thank you to everyone who has ever encouraged me to write this book. It's all your fault.

To Rachel Small, for her patience and ninja editing skills helping to turn my ramblings and musing into sentences, paragraphs, and chapters.

To 100covers for translating my unconnected brain farts into a coherent cover.

To my merry band of beta readers, who spotted and corrected those pesky misspellings, grammatical errors and sentences that made little sense. Thank you, Linda Moren Abuelghanam, Pauline Armstrong, Judith Benson, Liesbet Collaert, Julie Haigh, Eileen Kuriger Huestis, Susan Jackson, Simon Michael Prior, Irene Pylypec, Kyra Robinov, Alyson Sheldrake, and Lisa Rose Wright.

My Advanced Readers for taking the time to read and offer last-minute pieces of advice about the book. Thank you.

To L for your love and support and for putting up with my artistic outbursts.

Finally, to you, the reader, for taking the time to read my books. Long may it continue.

ABOUT THE AUTHOR

Kevin Kelly is the author of the Midlife Misadventures Comedy Travel Memoir series. He often hangs out on Facebook on his author page, posting memes, pictures. Click the Facebook link below.

Kevin is also a member of a fabulous group on Facebook for lovers of Memoir Books, the friendliest group on Facebook with loads of content, competitions, and chances to win and read books you'll love. You can find them

https://www.facebook.com/groups/welovememoirs

See you on the other side.

www.ingramcontent.com/pod-product-compliance
Lightning Source LLC
Chambersburg PA
CBHW021432080526
44588CB00009B/503